AF443654

What Makes Bosses Tick?

WHAT MAKES BOSSES TICK?

How to Cope with Them

Katherine Gant Maxwell, Ph.D.

VANTAGE PRESS
New York / Washington / Atlanta
Los Angeles / Chicago

FIRST EDITION

All rights reserved, including the right of
reproduction in whole or in part in any form.

Copyright © 1986 by Katherine Gant Maxwell, Ph.D.

Published by Vantage Press, Inc.
516 West 34th Street, New York, New York 10001

Manufactured in the United States of America
ISBN: 0-533-06680-8

Library of Congress Catalog Card No.: 85-90183

To my husband, Fowden Gene,
and my children:
Steve, Rebecca, and Randy

The revelations within this book are fictional. Resemblance to the history of any individual is strictly coincidental.

Names of characters, schools, and towns are entirely fictional; they do not currently exist, nor have they existed in the past, to my knowledge.

Katherine Gant Maxwell, Ph.D.

CONTENTS

What Makes Bosses Tick?

PART I
WHAT MAKES BOSSES TICK?

INTRODUCTION TO PART I

Part I contains information that it is hoped will assist the readers in better understanding key individuals in their lives—their bosses. The employers within Chapter I have what psychologists call personality problems. Their behavior is of a less severe degree than that which is found within the neurotic or psychotic individual. Chapter II consists of a description of a well-adjusted boss who reigns with a democratic hand.

With these thoughts in mind, let us now proceed through the following pages.

Chapter I

PERSONALITIES OF HARD-TO-HANDLE BOSSES

Bosses are interestingly located within diversified leadership settings, from the ivory, vine-covered walls of the noble university to the distant, tiny businesses lining the streets of an American city.

Employers come in different shapes, sizes, and heights, comprising a phenomenal array of unique personalities!

Bosses may quickly forget their days as employees, creating a void where once there was empathy. They are usually never bound by a code of ethics. Their whims and personalities may result either in a dictatorial, ironhanded rule or in one that is freedom-loving and democratic.

Bosses have usually advanced to their present positions through a liberal mixture of hard knocks and work. Many relish their status with sheer delight as they sit in their plush, executive chairs. In their righteous eyes, they occupy the most prestigious of positions.

Effective bosses with emotionally healthy personalities are as priceless as shiny gold, which skyrockets on the world stockmarket.

Pressure constantly bombards the core of leadership resulting from the urgent demands of the higher administration or from the peace-keeping task of preventing employees from quarreling. The manner in which these ever-present pressures are outwardly handled depends upon the leader's unique, inner, behavioral traits.

In the following pages there is a dissection of leadership

styles and behaviors of bosses with personality problems. These employers were—and still are—representative of those who are in diversified leadership positions. Therefore, information herein applies to bosses in general, regardless of the specific locations of their professional orientations.

A Boss with a Hysterical Personality

Bosses with a hysterical personality may have one or more of the following behaviors; the more of these characteristics in his/her personality, the more definitive the problem:

- Seeks attention;
- Likes to play a dramatizing role;
- Is vain, egocentric, and egotistical;
- Has shallow feelings;
- Is frequently seen as seductive and may behave in a sexually provocative way, using this as an attention-getting device;
- Overreacts to minor stresses with exaggerated emotional displays;
- Attempts to influence the behavior of colleagues and friends in order to meet some desired, self-imposed goal;
- Likes materialistic wealth;
- Places emphasis on making contact with important people upon whom he/she may rely to obtain a favored position;
- Masters the mechanics of obtaining the center of attention;
- Exhibits outward oppositon when it is safe;
- Avoids taking an unpopular stand;
- Depends heavily upon others for approval;
- Makes excessive demands on friends;
- Has immature ways of speaking and acting;
- Displays wishful thinking;
- When frustrated, can quickly become angry;
- May be impulsive and unreliable;
- Feels no need to be exact or on time;
- Will enter a social gathering late in order to make a dramatic entrance;

- Will purchase the most expensive home or car for impressive purposes;
- Lacks accuracy in his/her statements; for example, "That's what I meant and you should have known it.";
- Outward social appearance is important;
- Tends to imitate the behavior of those considered important;
- Places emphasis on being a member of the "inside group";
- Will exclude individuals who are different, looking at them with disdain;
- Seeks friends and cannot risk isolation;
- Usually friendly, social, and talkative; however, he/she may be shy, should the situation warrant it.
- Likes excitement and wants to be the center of it as long as there is no risk of uncomfortable consequences

PSYCHOLOGICALLY SPEAKING, WHAT MADE MRS. SOCIALITE TICK

With the previous characteristics tucked under our detective wing, we will now thoroughly explore—like a licensed, expertly qualified private investigator—Mrs. Socialite's behavior, innovatively finding justification for her stiff, socialized appearance. We will dig far below the extroverted, aggressive surface.

Mrs. Socialite was a middle-aged boss with a high-pitched, egotistical note in her precise voice. In appearance, she was consistently immaculately dressed with perfectly manicured nails. Her build was square and plump. Her strongly engraved features evidently had been gently fostered and painted by the wind and summer sun, producing darkly tanned skin.

Down under the recognizable, anxiety-ridden surface, Mrs. Socialite possessed an unacceptable dislike of herself—a trait intolerable in reality. She successfully obscured her interior being by assuming the air of a Hollywood actress, which served as a hypocritical buffer. She had unknowingly built a secure wall of self-protection around herself in an attempt to conceal her personality problems. It resembled a turtle's protective shell, which, with pending danger, could serve as an inner, secure haven, void of windows.

Mrs. Socialite's island of safety did permit access to numerous friends. However, she neatly excluded those who were in the least amount different.

In conversation, her words were icy, like icicles dangling from trees possessing needlelike tips whose stinging pierce contains a cutting quality. Her calmest words displayed a theatrical rage mixed with the mild aplomb of a natural politician—and masked her apparent, devilish intentions.

Mrs. Socialite, director of special education for Potpot Independent School District, had a key position. The dominant, existing problem was that she consistently remained well aware of this fact!

Mrs. Socialite had numerous attention-getting maneuvers, one of which was a time-consuming interviewing process for new personnel. The length of these extended ordeals averaged two weeks, during which every prospective employee was intensely interrogated.

A prime example supporting this valid fact were the probing assemblies conducted for the benefit of George, one of Mrs. Socialite's employees. Interviews with this boss were tests of endurance—difficult for the most stable of individuals.

Another of Mrs. Socialite's attention-getting devices was the weekly, sacredly reserved, Friday, all-day gathering of employees at which she sat cockily in charge, vauntingly displaying her narcissitic behavioral feathers. She resembled an arrogant rooster powerfully ruling his respectful flock of hens. Secret cries of numbed disgust were consistently mumbled about these time-deflating sessions by her employees.

Friday mornings were religiously set aside for vague group assemblies at which tons of worthless information—later quietly trash-canned—were distributed. At these sessions there were discussions of such momentous issues as forthcoming socials for school personnel and workshops for busy principals to alleviate their insufficient knowledge about special education. That these assemblies were abhorred was revealed by a lack of attendance.

The Friday-morning gathering was followed by a noon meeting conducted by a consulting, licensed, know-it-all psychologist who meticulously discussed emotionally disturbed students. Unfortunately—to the dismay of her employees—these behavioral treatises stimulated Mrs. Socialite into psychoanalyzing them. She quickly became infamous for her unorthodox interpretations of behavior!

Friday afternoons were utilized for what the subordinates nicknamed the "Torture Chamber Meetings." These provided a weekly opportunity for Mrs. Socialite and five of her administrative buddies to acrimoniously ridicule and rake fire and hail upon many of the heads of the employees. Whenever discovered, the smallest of problems or bungles was presented to this group. These self-declared experts sat in exalted prominence and judgment, resembling a jury waiting to condemn the guilty.

These weekly Torture Chamber Meetings consisted entirely of reprimands; they were absolutely void of compliments!

An example of the disgust that the employees secretly held can be found in a memorable occasion involving Timothy, an austere-looking man with an excessively calm manner. He had a clean-shaven, rigidly handsome face and was about five foot nine, solidly built with a strongly enforced gait. His voice was evenly modulated and low.

Timothy stormed hotheadedly from a Torture Chamber Meeting with every one of his small and large feathers ruffled. His entire facial expression was one of intense irritation, anger evident on every visible inch. He said, "I don't plan to take any more harassment from those horrible old hags. Boy, next time they make me mad, I'm gonna tell them where to head in"—and that was exactly what he did! However, his method of operation (MO) proved discouragingly futile, as he found himself standing in an unemployment line.

The employees dismayingly discovered that Friday—the most abhorred day of the week—and all its accompanying unpleasantness came with rapid reoccurrence—quick as the darting flashes of a Brownie Instamatic Camera. Without a doubt, had their desires been granted, Fridays would have been completely banned.

One afternoon during newly employed Lesta's first Torture Chamber Meeting, Mrs. Socialite smoothed out a nonexistent wrinkle in her immaculate, expertly well-fitted tan suit and tailored brown blouse. When summoned to the telephone, she cockily, authoritatively informed the group to continue. Lesta was the only one inexperienced enough to proceed. Although avowed members of the Torture Chamber Meeting were well indoctrinated to the fact, they refrained from advising him to presently remain silent until Mrs. Socialite's reentry. However, it did appear strange indeed to Lesta that the self-declared experts were not entering into the discussion.

Mrs. Socialite made her eloquent reappearance, strutting peacock-like, her face full of intense irritation and topped by a rigid frown. As she hotheadedly sat in her chair, her infuriation lapsed into silence as she rapped the table with consecutive fingers. Finally, her rage reached a cooler degree and she said with a surge of hostility, "Lesta, you haven't respected my authority. You went ahead without my presence."

"You said for us to continue. I was just doing what you indicated."

"Everyone knows not to proceed unless I'm here."

"I didn't mean to disobey you."

"But you did. That's unforgivable. I'll never forget this!"

The taut expression on Mrs. Socialite's face now exuded even more displeasure. Her face was, in every sense of the word, priceless. If her expression could have been entered into the Maddest Looking Face Contest, it would—without a doubt—have been victorious in landing first prize.

Mrs. Socialite's emotional disturbance was showing. Her hypocritical unpredictability had again erupted, resembling the characteristic heated fury of a massive volcano: one minute, it is shooting molten lava in every direction, and the next, it has reduced its furious force and lays dormant.

Each Torture Chamber Meeting erupted with a completely new set of discouraging dispatches. These messages resembled the reoccurring bad news of newscasters who seem compelled to convey totally droopy information—completely void of the least amount of cheerfulness.

On several occasions during Torture Chamber Meetings, employees casually presented suggestions for evaluation improvement. In every instance, they would attempt this one time, and one time alone! The caustic response from Mrs. Socialite significantly discouraged this type of maneuver. It was deemed by her as a caustic threat to her mighty empire, resembling—on a minute scale—the threat a country feels when its enemy invades its territorial borders.

It was obvious to her employees that Mrs. Socialite relished—in fact, demanded—that the "center-of-attention" spotlight be focused on her. Consistently, at both the Torture Chamber Meetings and other assemblies, she would religiously "steal the entire show." For these gatherings she would dress in a tight, sexually provocative dress. She would maneuver and swing her hips for the benefit of the males in attendance.

Mrs. Socialite's love of attention indicated significant immaturity, as she demanded the identical "limelight" she had enjoyed during childhood. Should there be a denial of this desire, sulking would immediately ensue.

Because of her attention-craving appetite, Mrs. Socialite relished sincere praise. However, attempts at flattery required top-notch honesty, for her sensitive perception could detect the least amount of fabrication—and, of course, this in and of itself could create a bigger bombshell than lavishing no praise at all.

Everything, absolutely everything—including doctor and dental appointments—required cancellation to pave the way for what Mrs. Socialite considered strategic: her socials. One employee described the situation beautifully when she said, "Hmmm . . . you know, in order to gain brownie points with Mrs. Socialite, it's good to volunteer at socials."

With experience, the employees discovered the expensive price of overt complaints. Two subordinates who had expressed disgruntled viewpoints found themselves standing, to their disgust, in the dreary, ego-deflating, unemployment line.

Although everyone, including teachers, social workers, and other school personnel, had access to her stuffed, gray metal file, her employees were held totally responsible for material therein which had been gleaned from their previous, individual schools. If anything was ever lost, they were bitterly accosted. An example of this was the day when Martie, one of the employees, vehemently complained to Mrs. Socialite with his firmest, tutorial voice (loaded with a pedagogic acrimony, lending support to his disgusted, inner feelings), "I lost a report for Chippy __ . I'm gonna have a devil of a time replacing it."

"That's inexcusable. We'll discuss this at your Friday meeting."

"But I couldn't help it."

"Oh, yes you could. You're not careful enough."

"Are we not allowed to make errors?"

"Stop arguing immediately—that is, unless you want to be fired." Mrs. Socialite's anger reached a high point at which time Martie's escape became urgent; he fled with the dazzling speed of an ostrich, a powerfully fast bird with excessively long legs, providing a swift flight.

When an agitated Martie returned to the cramped quarters of the employees, he quietly said, "I can't believe it. Old Lady Socialite feels we should be perfect; rather, that's what she just told me. This place is enough to give all of us ulcers."

Mrs. Socialite's hostility manifested itself in an outlandish, uncalled-for overreaction, easily stirred up by her employees, resembling an angry blue jay whose artistically colored feathers are modified to a vertical position when his territory is being invaded by a selfish intruder.

The employees within Mrs. Socialite's empire experienced yet another problem. Important papers containing irreplaceable signatures developed two legs, leading to their questionable flight out of sight. Her sheer devilment caused her to criticize the employees for misplaced papers. In fact, Mrs. Socialite found this a most enjoyable activity!

To conclude this treatise on Mrs. Socialite, let us look at the entire picture. Her domain could be likened to a dirty stream littered with trash, paper, rotted leaves, and empty, rusty cans which have floated to the top of the previously crystal-clear water, contaminating its purity. Also, her method of leadership, authoritative and depressing, was comparable to inclement weather such as mornings totally engulfed by thick, breathtaking, oppressive fog which persistently lingers, penetrating through warm, insulated jackets. Weather such as this creates excellent conditions for a car smashup. In addition, street signs vanish from visibility and become unreadable, even when in close proximity. The choking fog swallows the sounds of distant trains and the buzz of oncoming cars.

In conclusion to this section relative to Mrs. Socialite, in viewing her behavioral actions, it is possible to say that she had a hysterical personality. Her characteristics, which are indicative of this fact, include her desire for attention, tendencies to enter a social gathering late in order to make a dramatic entrance, the ability to quickly become angry, and to place an emphasis on her outward social appearance.

In retrospect, the overall picture depicts Mrs. Socialite's leadership style as authoritative. With her constant demand for attention, she did not grant one inch of freedom to her employees. Rather, she maintained the constant spotlight on herself.

A Boss with a Paranoid Personality

We will now examine the boss with a paranoid personality, who may display one or more of the following behaviors. The more of these characteristics in his/her personality, the more definitive the problem:

- Is defensive in order to protect himself/herself;
- Safeguards himself/herself against attack, either slight or large, imagined or real;
- Hypersensitive to slights (real or imagined);
- May magnify unconscious hostility in other people;
- May assume that that which is clear to him/her will be clear to others;
- Lacks basic trust and may be suspicious, jealous, and obstinate;
- Sees others as disliking him/her;
- Unable to tolerate criticism without resentment;

- Alert in his/her relationships with people for indications that will confirm his/her innate suspicion that others are out to get him/her;
- Makes few friends;
- Guards his/her private world;
- May utilize specific measures in order to protect himself/herself, like changing locks on doors, from time to time as a matter of precaution;
- Interpersonal relationships are usually unhappy;
- May be busy defending himself/herself and seems inconsiderate.

PSYCHOLOGICALLY SPEAKING, WHAT MADE MR. DICTA TICK

Let us now examine a fascinating boss with a paranoid personality, as depicted by Mr. Dicta, who—like Mrs. Socialite—was a director of special education. His appearance revealed a black, Hitler-like mustache, dark forbidding eyes, and strong, rigid, facial features.

Most prominent about Mr. Dicta was his powerful use of words—words that could provoke animosity in the ears of the listener. His utterings were totally negative. Employees inauspiciously received the verbal blows that he consistently rendered. Compliments were completely absent from his repertoire of overt speech.

Another method utilized by Mr. Dicta was a propaganda trail, consisting of coercive power spiced with scare tactics. This invaded the employees' main office with such exertion that they were forced into submissive roles. Psychologically, these individuals were compelled, through absolute allegiance, to essentially dissolve and subdue their own feelings and personalities, providing Mr. Dicta with complete control.

This boss totally assumed responsibility for main-office decisions. This burden took its toll by adding an additional level of tension to his already high-strung temperament. This problem was compounded by his threatened feelings, which erupted when excellent knowledge was conveyed or demonstrated by employees. An example of this was the retaliation received by one employee when she said to Mr. Dicta, "I've found out about a good method. It can be used for testing special-education students."

"Our system is already excellent. I don't appreciate your implication that what we use isn't good enough."

"I didn't mean this as an insult."

"Oh, yes, you did—and boy, I don't like this one bit."

"I apologize."

"I won't accept it. What's more, I'll not forget this infringement either."

The previous conversation is illustrative of Mr. Dicta's reactions on numerous occasions when his suspicious behavioral reactions erupted on the surface as a result of envisioning unjustified threats.

Accompanying Mr. Dicta's suspicions was his psychological mechanism of *projection*. Numerous psychologists describe this phenomenon as exhibited when the behavior of other individuals is interpreted within the confines of a person's view of himself/herself. Therefore, if individuals have erroneous views about their own actions or hate a specific trait, they may, in turn, project these qualities upon other humans.

Applying the above to Mr. Dicta, he continually projected his own detested attributes, whenever possible, to other individuals, especially those he disliked.

Mr. Dicta's previously discussed characteristics created in him a sensitive disposition. His hypersensitivity could be ignited with the touch of one, innocently spoken word. His employees remained on constant guard, eliminating specific, chattered, verbal expressions that might offend his fragile supersensitive shell.

The people composing Mr. Dicta's staff quickly yielded to his dominating commands in fear of losing their jobs. This submission was appealingly soothing to his chauvinistic, dictatorial feathers. It also eliminated the least amount of freedom for his employees, freedom being a concept he could not tolerate.

Anger—religiously igniting itself—remained at the forefront of Mr. Dicta's personality. His icy words provoked animosity in his subordinates, who were well aware that should he explode, the result would disastrously plaster his entire office, affecting everyone in the vicinity. When his anger surfaced, Mr. Dicta would glare at the innocent offender with one of his devilish stares, exhibiting a deeply etched furrow in his forehead. His two, fierce, black eyes glared with bitterness. His total state of angry shock typically caused his mustache to twitch at both ends. At such times, his resemblance to Hitler increased to a stronger degree. Mr. Dicta's anger made his employees feel like poor, trapped, frail mice staring into the eyes of an overpowering cat whose every thought contained visions of pouncing. His anger resembled a tropical storm with giant waves lashing against a rocky shore; it resembled the rage displayed by a charging bull as he tenaciously attempts to undermine the threatening, tantalizing red blanket of the bullfighter; it resembled the same heated frenzy of a tomcat whose territory is being invaded by another envious male cat.

Mr. Dicta had a disastrous habit of stereotyping employees. On numerous occasions he would rigidly stamp them with incorrect descriptions. These, in turn, grew with added embellishments until the initial picture had been entirely lost, shattered into a plurality of pieces containing misinterpretations of the truth—totally devastating to an individual's professional reputation.

In conclusion of this section relative to Mr. Dicta, in viewing his behavioral actions, it is possible to say that he had a paranoid personality. His characteristics, which are indicative of this fact, include the following: used propaganda; forced employees to be submissive; felt threatened; used projection, donating his undesirable traits to his employees; stereotyped employees; and was hypersensitive.

It is pertinent at this time to describe Mr. Dicta's leadership style. Because of his suspicious nature, this obnoxious boss put a clamp of security upon his entire domain. As a result, no amount of freedom was granted to his employees to exhibit leadership or accept other responsibilities. Therefore his leadership style was dictatorial and authoritative. Additional excellent material about the authoritarian personality can be found in the classic study, *The Authoritarian Personality*, by T.W. Adorno, Else Frenkel-Brunswik, Daniel J. Levinson, and R. Nevitt Sanford.

A Boss with an Obsessive-Compulsive Personality

We will now examine the boss with an obsessive-compulsive personality, who may exhibit one or more of the following behaviors. The more of these characteristics in his/her personality, the more definitive the problem:

- Has an excessive need for conformity;
- May be rigid;
- May be overconscientious;
- May not be able to relax easily;
- May dislike unclear and unpredictable situations;
- Unpredictable conditions may create anxiety within him/her;
- Likes to organize his/her life down to the smallest of details;
- Prefers not to take chances;
- Prefers to plan ahead of time and not leave things until the last minute;
- May see himself/herself as responsible for what happens;
- Feels the desperate need to control his/her environment as well as himself/herself;
- Feels anxiety when things are out of control;
- Rituals may be appealing and he/she may utilize this technique for controlling his/her world, such as religiously checking time and again a stack of papers to determine that things are in order;
- Tries to be correct, striving for perfection;

- May analyze and examine tiny statements in an argument in order to protect himself/herself;
- Works better in a structured, organized environment where he/she can maintain control;
- If his/her situation depends on the tempermental mood changes of his/her boss, he/she may become anxious and fearful;
- May offend employees because of his/her extreme attention to detail;
- Is unable to delegate responsibility, feeling the compulsive need to do everything himself/herself;
- Is a hard worker who may outwardly seem trustworthy and responsible;
- Expects perfection from his/her employees;
- Has workaholic tendencies.

PSYCHOLOGICALLY SPEAKING, WHAT MADE BELL TICK

With the previous characteristics in the mind's eye of the reader, we will now discuss our next boss, Bell, also a director of special education. A lady in her middle thirties, excessively overweight, she was uniquely interesting in her own way. Had a minute portion of the layers of fat been removed from her face, a thing of beauty would have emerged. Rounding out her appearance was a neighborly expression consisting of a blue-eyed, glassy stare topped off with short, golden-brown hair. Her typical dresses were tight fitting—an attempt to reproportion her figure into a shapely form.

The most obvious characteristic prevailing in the atmosphere in Bell's tour of duty was an obsessive-compulsive, overreactive, personality drive creating a confusion-instilling air in the unsuspecting minds of her recipients. This condition endured the entire year as she impulsively and quickly jumped from one situation to another. One task would remain incomplete as numerous others would intermittently develop. Suffering from her confused mess most intensely were her employees, who consistently felt they were in the midst of a tornado pouring out its fury on Mother Earth.

The force of Bell's driving personality with its total domination of administrative council meetings had impulsively repelled her colleagues, dressed as they were in the human skins of principals and superintendents. The chief criticism stemmed from her attempt to immediately force her excellent ideas and new programs down the throats of her victims regardless of the present wishes and desires of her colleagues. These gentlemen would have assuredly disliked such domination from a man, but from a woman it was absolutely intolerable.

Bell's dictatorial rule had caused her to be fired at the end of the year. And, of course, she dominately disagreed with this decision!

The following conversation between two principals beautifully describes the situation.

"Bell has never left room for principals to feel the least bit a part of pending regulations. This shouldn't be the case."

"She always makes every decision before we go to an administrative council meeting. Then we sit there and listen as the whole mess is crammed down our throats."

"She's the worst director of special education we've ever had. I'm sick and tired of her stealing the entire show."

"Me, too."

"Seems like she has to have strict control of everything or else she's miserable."

This last divulging statement delves into the heart of the problem. It befittingly describes one of the main problems of an obsessive-compulsive individual.

Bell had totally bypassed every rule of the administrative game. A victorious, professional relationship would have been one of compatibility spiced with mutual harmony, with neither the director of special education nor the administrators faithfully governing the unqualified scene.

Bell's overreactive environment set this stage for her employment world. Her employees were consistently influenced to perform likewise. Therefore, the entire work arena remained in a state of disruptive tension.

If ever questioned by employees in regard to her self-imposed regulations, Bell's rage and fury would reach a massive, explosive stage of volcanic force, wielding its influence for numerous weeks. This was due, in part, to her inability to forget infringements—whether imagined or real. It was typical for her hysterical anger to rise if anyone—even to a minute degree—dissented with her decisions. Employees were well aware of the impossibility of changing her rigid mind!

A dominant trait possessed by Bell was her inability to accept a lack of what she considered sole allegiance from her employees. Should there be deflection, in the least, from her prevailing authority, it was met by severe reprimands heaped upon the head of the involved employee.

Another of Bell's noticeable traits was a tendency to gossip during the noon hour. Although the food was as delicious as a home-cooked meal, with the piping hot, huge, freshly baked rolls with delicately flavored butter spilling over their edges, it was difficult for her employees dining at the same table to devote full concentration on their meal because of Bell's bitter monologues. Her employees found their food disappeared rapidly, but it was depleted hastily with hardly a taste, in order to escape. Bell's gossip ruined many an otherwise elegant meal. Her chatter was fierce, causing her to frequently choke on a mouthful of food. These monologues often divulged the tremendous and unfortunate ordeals that she had endured during the previous year. In addition, she was devoted to her favorite subject: her dismissal.

Bell also ripped her colleagues asunder with fitful vengeance, enriching every breath with curses. These offensive noon sessions sounded like a cacklehouse inhabited by a bunch of gossipy hens chattering their feathered lives away. These manifest discussions were situated in local restaurants with tones exclamatory enough for enjoyment of other noontime clientele.

Not only did Bell converse on her favorite subject during the noon hour, but also during working hours, and as a result, her employees could not complete their tasks. Instead, her obnoxious topic filled with filthy lies of damaging proportions was forced upon them as Bell restlessly paced from work station to work station on the hard, wooden floor, wearing down its surface with her repeated, stomping steps.

Bell's every word could distinctly, with pungency and ambidexterity, be heard by workplace occupants—the innocent recipients of her offensive testimonies. Muffling one's involuntarily receptive ears proved to be ineffective during these caustic outpourings. In many respects, Bell's gossip resembled a grass fire which rapidly spreads with impending force until its fury has burned all the existing, living vegetation within its path.

Bell encouraged one employee to disgustingly invade into the territorial arena of another. This behavior fostered in her employees a willingness to take sides in involved issues or decisions.

Bell's search for perfection would not allow errors to be made by her employees. Whenever mistakes crept in, she was unforgiving. The involved employee would be daily reminded of the infringement. In addition, Bell spent significant time determining that her employees' work remained error-free. She persistently, thoroughly, examined tons of paperwork. Fortunately, her employees saw the humor inherent therein as they silently snickered, "We should feel honored indeed for this devoted attention."

Bell could have handled her existent pressure in one of three ways: (1) by an inward exertion causing bleeding ulcers or other stress-related illnesses; (2) by a healthy means with neither inward nor outward lashing; or (3) by direction toward an outer source—a *scapegoat* who catches fire and hail for errors that are not rightfully his/hers to accept.

The last one was displayed in a straightforward manner by Bell. She directed her bitter pressure-lashing at convenient, accessible, and available sources—*scapegoats*, who proved to be her innocent employees.

The delicate fuse of Bell's belligerent time-bomb was easily lighted. The fuel behind the ignition remained subconsciously hidden within her. Its force resulted from the accumulated strain and tension that she had suffered for months—tension of her own making.

At the conclusion of school, the reason behind her termination promptly became evident. Loud proclamations of disapproval—which rang clear and demanding—were heard from the smallest to the largest school. These widespread gossipy rumblings gave a powerful indication of the indelible, infamous mark Bell had left. Her reign had infuriated school personnel, who now seethed with bitter thoughts of this obnoxious human.

To conclude this discussion of Bell, let us view the entire picture. Her confusion left a trail of disgruntled school personnel. The situation resembled a massive whirlwind in which debris is thrown asunder. However, instead of garbage, it was the professional lives of Bell's colleagues and her employees that were affected.

In summary of this section relative to Bell, her personality could be described as an obsessive-compulsive one with the following behavioral characteristics: caused confusion as she jumped from one task to another; was domineering, unwilling to delegate authority; had to have strict control; had a tendency to overreact.

In addition, a view of Bell's leadership style indicated that she was exerting an authoritarian hold on her employees. Since her personality demanded a rigid control over every aspect of her life, this same tendency held true in the professional arena as well.

A Boss with a Schizoid Personality

We will now examine the boss with a schizoid personality, who may exhibit one or more of the following behaviors. The more of these characteristics in his/her personality, the more definitive the problem:

• Seems to be a "loner" and is seclusive, with little desire for

companionship; has a tendency to avoid close or prolonged relationships;
- Doesn't expect to find a real place in the social world, retreating from it to some private corner; functions as a social isolate, as if he/she were trying to shelter himself/herself from others;
- Seems aloof and disinterested;
- Appears to live in an ivory tower; a detached and abstract thinker;
- Uncomfortable with others;
- Excessive time may be spent daydreaming;
- Cannot express hostility;
- Unsatisfying to hold a conversation with him/her for he/she makes little effort to keep the communication going;
- Is secretive and does not talk about himself/herself, in order to maintain his/her privacy;
- Never feels fully accepted;
- Avoids competitive relationships;
- Appears odd or snobbish;
- May give the appearance of being self-sufficient;
- May become a recluse who lives in a little room and seldom speaks to anyone;
- Especially uncomfortable around members of the opposite sex; seldom dates.

PSYCHOLOGICALLY SPEAKING, WHAT MADE TOMMY TICK

Tommy, a boss with a schizoid personality, was a fascinating and interesting mixture of behavioral characteristics. In appearance, he was a tall, neatly dressed, handsome gentleman with a solemn, expressionless face—one which never smiled, seeming to foretell the unhappy disposition housed within his inner subconscious.

With his own peculiarities, Tommy maintained his employer role through his self-employment because he owned a manufacturing company.

It was obvious to Tommy's employees that he typically

avoided close relationships, never engaging in socials or even in coffee breaks. Soft whispers of complaints could be heard from his employees with descriptions of their boss's aloof, snobbish, disinterested, and detached attitude.

When viewing Tommy at close range, he was significantly uncomfortable in the presence of other individuals. This was made obvious by his twitching face and nervously moving eyes and body. These traits were especially recognizable at meetings and whenever public speaking was required. Only out of necessity did Tommy ever volunteer a minute word in group participations.

On one occasion when talking with an employee, Tommy vividly expressed his feelings: "I'm ill at ease and intentionally avoid social affairs. I also don't like meetings where I feel obligated to talk."

At Christmastime, Tommy's employees graciously invited him to privately planned parties. However, he consistently, hesitatingly replied, "I've got a conflict. I will not be able to come." This was an avoidance maneuver for escaping a painful situation.

It was obvious that Tommy totally avoided entering into competitions. Several of his male colleagues had approached him about joining a softball league. They had discovered, during an interesting investigation, that he had been an excellent pitcher when in high school. However, Tommy refused their invitation.

Tommy was a secretive individual, closely guarding anything related to his personal life. He retreated into a safe, private corner like a bear who goes into hibernation during the winter months—completely withdrawing from view.

With but one exception relating to competitions, Tommy was unable to express hostility, never exhibiting anger, nor even justified wrath. This was puzzling to both colleagues and subordinates.

Complaints were voiced by his employees when expressing difficulty in understanding where they stood in the total professional picture. They completely lacked sufficient job descriptions which created an uncomfortable position, along with its ensuing confusion.

Tommy exhibited very little concern about making strategic decisions, thereby maintaining the status quo of his employees' progress.

In conclusion to this section relative to Tommy, in viewing his behavioral actions, it is possible to say that he had a schizoid personality. His characteristics, which are indicative of this fact, include the following: Tommy made little effort to keep a conversation progressing; never felt fully accepted; avoided social events; avoided competitive events; was secretive and closely guarded his personal life; and appeared aloof and snobbish.

This boss had a tendency to consistently exert leadership within the *laissez-faire* realm, with a "I don't care" attitude. His style was neither dictatorial nor democratic.

A Boss with a Manic-Depressive Personality

We will now examine the boss with a manic-depressive personality, who may have one or more of the following traits. The more of these characteristics in his/her personality, the more definitive the problem:

- Switches quickly from a mood that is enthusiastic and optimistic to one that is grouchy and depressed;
- Inconsistently temperamental;
- Difficult to judge from one day to the next what mood will be displayed;
- Following a tense situation, he/she may become excessively elated and happy;
- May, at times, be easily distracted; not an adequate listener;
- May, at times, be unable to remain with a task for a lengthy period of time, instead remains in a constant state of shifting from one task to another;
- May, at times, shout very loudly and excitedly when talking to another individual, either in person or over the telephone;
- May, at times, overreact when such a strong display of emotion is not justified;
- May, at times, be excessively talkative, creating difficulty for

another person attempting to enter into the converstion;
- May, at times, jump from one topic to another;
- His/her above behaviors do not correspond to the appropriate situations, either at work or in a social setting.

PSYCHOLOGICALLY SPEAKING, WHAT MADE LOU TICK

A perfect object of study for the manic-depressive personality is Lou, a relatively young woman with blond hair, blue eyes, of average size and height, who possessed the unusual characteristic of quickly changing expressions from smiling eyes and mouth to an opposing angry scowl.

Lou was self-employed. She owned a restaurant in which she had five employees.

It was an acknowledged impossibility to predict from one day to the next which temperamental mood Lou would exhibit. At intervals she would enter her professional arena with an ambitious, enthusiastic, and optimistic attitude, welcoming new ideas or plans furnished by her employees. However, within hours Lou had the capacity to express bitter disdain for the previously accepted piece of effective planning.

On several instances during an employee strategy meeting, she demonstrated ambivalence—liking the project one hour but voicing disapproval the next.

Lou's employees were concerned about her moodiness. Without prior warning, during the same day or else on a consecutively new one, her mood would change from a happy, warm disposition to one of apparent depression. Her changeable personality was comparable to the spring weather which is full of sunshine one moment and full of dreary rain the next.

In conclusion to this section relative to Lou, in viewing her behavioral actions, it is possible to say that she had a manic-depressive personality. Her characteristics, which are indicative of this fact, include the following: would quickly change her behavior from cheerful and sunny to one of depression, and would become moody during specific intervals.

Lou's leadership style swung from democratic to dictatorial, depending upon which mood she exhibited. Her optimistic mood brought into existence democratic leadership, while—in contrast—her depressed mood immediately sent her into the throes of a dictatorship. Her employees remained massively confused the majority of the time, trying to predict whether they had the freedom to function within the democratic sphere or whether they must conform to a complete dictatorship.

A Boss with an Inadequate Personality

We will now dissect the boss with an inadequate personality who may demonstrate one or more of the following behaviors. The more of these characteristics in his/her personality, the more definitive the problem:

- May give inappropriate responses to emotional, social, and physical demands at work;
- May display inadaptability and lack of responsibility;
- May use poor judgment;
- May lack physical stamina;
- May cause himself/herself or others to fail at some task.

PSYCHOLOGICALLY SPEAKING, WHAT MADE JOLYDA TICK

Jolyda was self-employed and owned an antique store. In appearance, she had a thin crop of gray, tailored, straight, short hair with girlish, immature bangs. Completing a description of her physical attributes were blue eyes and a short, plump, middle-aged–plus, spreading figure. Topping off these characteristics was a childlike voice which ranged all the way up to a high-pitched crescendo.

Jolyda's unhappy employees justifiably, with whispers of disgust, complained. They were disgruntled because of the lack of responsibility their leader showed. This tendency evolved from a mixture of leftover immaturity, difficulty in adapting, and selfishness during her previous days of childhood.

To conclude this section on Jolyda, she could be described as having an inadequate personality, indicated by her lack of shouldering responsibility. Because her behavioral traits created a stagnating working environment, Jolyda had a high turnover of employees. They experienced difficulty laboring under her supervisory wing.

Jolyda's leadership existed more within the *laissez-faire* realm—it was neither dictatorial nor democratic. She cared neither one way nor the other whether responsibilities were fulfilled. In fact, she made a seemingly conscientious effort to avoid them. In this regard, she manifested the maturity level of a preteenager.

Chapter II

THE DEMOCRATIC BOSS (A BOSS WITH A WELL-ADJUSTED PERSONALITY)

Positive attitudes are dynamic! They are winners! These words beautifully describe the democratic employer. For this type of administrator, looming shadows do not silently lurk behind advancing corners. Radiant sunshine, with its glory, spreads rapidly into the precious, inner soul of this employer. A cheerful expression appears on the face of this leader—the individual with a positive attitude!

Numerous democratic leaders have weathered professional storms, tenaciously climbing the employment ladder. They have strongly coped with both challenges and impossible hurdles.

Priceless indeed is the democratic employer's positive outlook—free from overreactive sensitivity, free from unfounded suspicions, free from the mental prison which can hold its owner behind immovable bars, free from inner, dark dungeons of depressing despair.

The positive attitudes of democratic administrators effectively insulate and protect them from criticisms and unjustified insults. These attitudes reinforce them with added strength and abilities.

The previous description beautifully describes Mr. Bow, the democratic boss we will discuss in this chapter. He was a gentleman in his late forties, with blue eyes and closely cropped, blonde hair streaked with visible traces of gray.

Mr. Bow was a master of hiring capable individuals upon whom he bestowed all the responsibilities of their positions. At no time did he ever infringe upon the professional jurisdiction of his employees, granting them an unlimited freedom to function within their individual roles.

This democratic leader possessed a friendly, reassuring disposition combined with the ability to establish a feeling of ease within his visitors. Examples of this were continuously demonstrated during interviews with prospective employees. At these times, he established stars of hope—stars whose positive rays twinkled from his personality, stars whose light dispersed negative shadows into oblivion.

Newly employed faculty were thoroughly briefed on every aspect of their positions. None of these individuals were stranded, groping for their way—for their paths were excellently carved by Mr. Bow.

This democratic leader was a master at effective communication, for he used properly delivered words—words that had a binding quality like the written, legal documents of attorneys; words that had comforting qualities, like those created by beautiful musical lyrics; words that had healing qualities, drawing his faculty closer; words that had strategic power, like those of an army general; words that had the eloquence of an arbitrator who can temper the sharpest of disgruntled conversations; words that were as gorgeous as a radiantly blooming orchid in all its magnificent splendor.

It was obvious that Mr. Bow's faculty meetings manifested elaborate organization and preplanning. They were superb—to put it mildly! At these meetings, this effective administrator tactfully and skillfully disposed of irrelevant ideas. For example, there was one teacher, Lily, who was obviously guilty of this obnoxious problem of bringing up unimportant issues. Also manifestly apparent was her motive: she desired excessive attention. She rendered many an impertinent idea, which flowed from her unhealthy mouth like energetic Coke spurting from a shaken-up can, covering the recipient with its sprayed force. However, in one particular situation, the unfortunate receivers were Mr. Bow and his employees, disgustingly besieged by her objectionable actions.

An effective lid was clamped on Lily's mouth, which resembled the sealant ability of strapping tape which is placed on packages to be mailed. Mr. Bow's method of operation (MO) of politely, assertively, confidentially informing Lily to either shut up or ship out proved effective and was assuredly a relief to his faculty! In this regard, he had been as wise as an owl and as innovatively resourceful as an energetic beaver who skillfully plans the construction of a complex dam, which could easily compare favorably with the most majestic of human engineering endeavors.

Mr. Bow consistently and obviously manifested a superb, intelligent philosophy of open communication, with decisions based—whenever possible—on the faculty's thoughts. As a result, there evolved a sense of loyal identity and a willingness to cooperate with this democratic leader at the helm, guiding and coordinating the decision-making process.

It quickly became obvious to new faculty that Mr. Bow wore numerous, unique, professional hats: director of special education for the Hurrah Cooperative (Coop) Independent School District, director of curriculum, supervisor of teaching, supervisor of principals and superintendents. He efficiently carried out the responsibilities of four administrators—a priceless and irreplaceable jewel of leadership!

This democratic leader was endowed with excellent capacity to rejuvenate energy—energy resembling that of the powerful sun which bestows life into vegetation by utilizing a miraculous, photosynthetic method. Through this technique, luscious, green plants systematically convert the sun's life-giving force into nourishing carbohydrates. The faculty—like a fertile plant—absorbed the metabolic satisfaction generated by Mr. Bow's encouraging environment, satisfaction which proceeded from their brain's sunshine-filled emotional centers and moved—like carbohydrates in the plant—to every portion of their classrooms.

Among earthly blessings, nothing—absolutely nothing—was as priceless and powerful as Mr. Bow's enriching environment, which contained a phenomenal, pliable web of strength that reinforced the fortunate faculty and poured into every crevice of the independent school district.

In addition to this democratic leader's other admirable qualities, he exhibited a fantastic listening ability, evident on one occasion when a fourth-grade teacher conferred with him while on the playground. She interrogated him about the advisability of utilizing specific workbooks in her special-education classroom. Mr. Bow, realizing his inability to skillfully listen at this time, requested that the teacher make an appointment in order to discuss this subject in a better location.

Because of this powerful leader's influence, peace existed within the Hurrah Coop. A path of inner solitude had been paved over throughout the years by the patience, fortitude, and excellent vision of school administrators, especially including Mr. Bow.

With a democratic leader's superb efficiency, Mr. Bow executed responsibilities spiced with a marvelous sense of direction, which rescued him from useless work. His management expertise resembled the magnificent, smooth-running operation of the complex, human body, in which every minute part is coordinated to perfection with the others.

Never did this democratic leader make his teachers appear stupid or guilty for supplying an idea. His generously acceptant attitude was like an audience of opera lovers whose applause rapturously encourages the musical artist. As the listeners richly receive the melodious music, likewise Mr. Bow received suggestions from his faculty.

Mr. Bow artfully handled the most difficult of conferences, which consistently ended on a smooth note as eloquent as the music of the gifted pianist on the concert stage—but, of course, everything he did ran with top-notch organization!

This democratic administrator consistently supplied adequate guidance, maintaining precise, efficiently balanced participation between cooperative and competitive faculty. For example, he silenced a heated quarrel involving two faculty members with opposing viewpoints, softening the verbal blows coming from the aggressive instigator of the troublesome situation.

One of the most admirable of Mr. Bow's traits was his beautiful gift of trust and faith in his faculty. He graciously accepted—without insults or questioned suspicions—teachers' accidental errors. His trust resembled that which a child feels for his excellent parents, never doubting for one moment their overt behavioral actions. This democratic leader's gift of belief in humanity was richly valuable, richly enduring, and richly radiant, spreading to the far corners of the Hurrah Coop.

Through Mr. Bow's influence, cooperation existed among his teachers—comparable to a basketball team that wins the game through joint, loyal participation. He was always able to quench lighted fires of anger which arose at infrequent intervals.

This democratic leader's method of operation (MO) for settling disputes was truly amazing. For example, he would individually see the involved employees; then a collective gathering transpired.

The sheer happiness that the faculty possessed was likened to that felt by a Florida tropical songbird who jubilantly warbles delicately toned notes to convey his thanksgiving for life itself, for delicious meals of insects or worms, for his home nest of twigs and branches, and for the luscious gift of the mild Florida winters. These, in themselves, prevented the bird's task of moving to escape the cold of winter.

Hurrah Coop faculty thrived under the superb, democratic leadership style which did—beyond question—stimulate independence of the professionals working for Mr. Bow. Psychologically, his effective methods could be literally described as group- as opposed to leader-centered.

Another of Mr. Bow's positive attributes was the manner in which he guided his faculty by suggestion, rather than by domineeringly exerting pressure. His faculty could well be compared to eagles that are granted complete freedom of flight to gracefully, mightily soar in the vast expanse of blue sky.

A loyal community spirit was evident in the Hurrah Coop. It resembled the rigid stability of Elmer's glue which tightly bonds two sheets of paper. As the glue secures the paper, likewise was the loyalty of faculty bound to the school.

Not often—but periodically—one of the faculty made Mr.

Bow angry. The reasons were always completely legitimate. One example was the time when Harry and Bill became involved in a bitterly outrageous fight. Angry temperatures had reached the level of outright, tenacious, physical blows. These teachers saw Mr. Bow in an extended conference at which time the fire was totally eliminated!

Another interval when Mr. Bow's temper was justifiably kindled was in the following situation: Two high-school teachers were taking advantage of their coffee breaks and leaving the school premises for an extended period. The principal had been unable to rectify the problem. However, no such problem was experienced by Mr. Bow who, with his usual firm, effective leadership, quickly corrected the problem. He informed them that they should either rectify the situation or be dismissed.

Mr. Bow had a superb self-concept level, a mechanism which is strategically crucial. It contains maneuverability qualities, as it directs the full range of an individual's behavior. It can be likened to the engine of a train which has absolute power to move the cars in whichever way it desires.

This democratic leader assisted his school personnel in improving their professional positions. For example, he would submit names of excellent teachers for the state competition for superior teacher of the year. The Hurrah Coop was famous for receiving this recognition!

This democratic leader also knowledgeably understood the psychology of complex oddities which comprise humans. An example of this point occurred when Mr. Bow's secretary and his bookkeeper became embroiled in a heated argument. Their irritated tones became louder and more distinct until they reached the far corners of the entire building. With Mr. Bow's assistance, these two realized that jealousy was instigating their behavior. He again effectively squelched the explosion!

Another of Mr. Bow's positive traits was evident in the form of sincere compliments. These could be compared to received Christmas gifts that were purchased sacrificiously by a loving heart. His praises to employees were gifts that were far more priceless than rubies or emeralds!

Although this democratic leader had sufficient knowledge,

an abundance of experience, and was satisfactorily versed on the mechanics of his professional position, he continually detected when he needed augmented information. His beautiful attitude of relying on his employees' areas of expertise was like a crystal-clear, mountain creek which relies on the natural springs for its life-giving water.

Another of Mr. Bow's positive attributes was social awareness. He expressed sympathy during deaths or other traumatic situations involving his faculty.

High on this democratic leader's list of remarkable traits was his support of deserving faculty. An example was the interval when he was in a special-education workship discussing placement of a mentally retarded eighth grader. In barged an ill-humored parent with Mr. Bow's secretary trailing behind and unable to stop her. Without stopping to catch her breath, the parent stormily presented a plurality of accusations about a certain teacher to which he was forced to listen—due to the fact that he could not get in so much as one word.

The parent's mighty gush of foul words slackened, presenting Mr. Bow with an opportunity to suggest that she come in for a conference. She accepted this offer!

After her exit, Mr. Bow declared that he would protect the rights of the involved teacher. He proclaimed her as an expert in her field and deserving of protection.

In addition to this democratic administrator's other superior qualities, he quickly saw the humor in situations. Whether related or not to his obvious actions, he remained ever aware of the power of humor. An example of this was the early morning event when he quiescently—a typical characteristic—entered his secretary's cheerfully painted office. He had something protruding from one of his brown suit's pant legs. The secretary, Jerrie, pointed to the unusual object. Upon observing the situation, Mr. Bow pulled on the tan cloth. Out gracefully came a woman's panty hose. He then laughed with one of his gleeful exhilarations, and commented, "That's one of my wife's pair of hose. Jumped into that pant leg during the washing."

At that point, Mr. Bow thought of another humorous situation. A wide smile spread across his handsome face as he laughingly said, "Let me tell you what happened to me last week. I was making a talk at this businessmen's luncheon. I was standing on a narrow, elevated platform. Uh . . . after my speech, I stepped backward and completely fell off the crazy thing. The audience was in . . . in absolute silence—until I came crawling back up to the podium! When they saw I wasn't hurt, they all started laughing."

Faculty members of the Hurrah Coop were richly blessed! Their lives were full of enrichment, full of purpose, full of happiness, and full of visible goals. Their professional lives had been beautifully woven into the school's educational fabric!

At the end of each year, this democratic leader determined if faculty replacements were needed for the following year. Few, if any, usually surfaced. However, new recruits were examined by Mr. Bow for the essential qualities of comprehension, intelligence, education, emotional stability, personal commitment, and a range of interests—qualities that would preserve his already established professionalism in his environment.

The enthusiasm felt by employees in the Hurrah Coop consistently spread from one to another, resembling the chain reaction of 100 meticulously placed dominoes. When the first one falls and touches the second, it likewise falls. As each one is touched, this causes a chain-reactive effect, with a synchronization of the plastic, black dominoes falling gracefully in a rhythmical pattern.

At the beginning of each Hurrah Coop school year, excitement broadcasted itself through the air—excitement stemming from invigorated students and rested school personnel who were ready for a new pace, who possessed alert, rejuvenated brains, and whose faces glowed from their inner, revived vigor. They were glad to be back working under Mr. Bow's supervision!

Working in the Hurrah Coop with Mr. Bow's positive attitude made life absolutely beautiful. This experience was like the description found in an elegantly written book whose every page conveys a rapture, a glory, depicting its inner contents. Like the book that has a gorgeously electrifying story to tell, blissfully beaming from cover to cover, likewise did lives encompassed within this calm atmosphere feel the glory of this situation radiantly transferred.

Mr. Bow's leadership was priceless—irreplaceable!

PART II
COPING WITH
HARD-TO-HANDLE BOSSES

INTRODUCTION TO PART II

Let us focus at this time on how one can effectively cope with a difficult boss. Learning to cope or understand a boss will enable you to function more effectively in a frustrating work environment, relieve stress, and as a result enjoy your job better. You will thus be a more happy and fulfilled individual. It will give you strength comparable to that of an active battery which provides power for a smooth-running Oldsmobile.

Chapter III

EMPLOYMENT COPING KEYS

The coping mechanisms described in this chapter will help you adjust to a disagreeable boss. Overcoming problems and difficulties with this type of individual is entirely possible. It will require a constant effort resembling the exertions of a tiny tugboat which persistently maneuvers the powerful ship.

As soon as it is suspected that your employer will create problems, immediately—with the swiftness of a kangaroo's leap—take steps to adequately cope with your problem. If you prefer not to resign, then apply the following coping keys for adjustment purposes. Hopefully, these will help you in the adverse employment world with its resulting multitude of frustrations pouring down like hot, molten lead from a car manufacturer's electrical machine.

Coping Key Number One: Laughter

Laughter is excellent medicine. It is a life-sustaining force as curing as the Bufferin that chases the migraine headache into oblivion!

Laughter can remediate various kinds of problems: it can change a dreary day into one of beauty; it can turn depressed individuals into ones who are delightful to be around; it can cure the woes of the three *D*s: *d*epression, *d*iscouragement, and *d*isenchantment.

Conduct a full-scale research investigation with the quality of laughter as a technique, hopefully bringing about a change in your boss. The next time your employer is grumpy as a one hundred-year–old great-grandpa, happily respond to his/her requests. You may be lucky enough to change him/her into a congenial employer who will see and appreciate a happy employee.

Quit taking yourself seriously. Laugh at your mistakes, for they are humanly impossible to avoid, regardless of the degree of perfection incorporated. These are as normal as the typing errors of the expert specialist in front of the typewriter. Laughing at yourself will relieve a portion of the stress you feel and chase away the rainy-day blues.

Coping Key Number Two: Understanding Yourself

Study yourself like the psychological research scientist who investigates the hyperactivity of the preschool child. Realize that snugly within you lies the ability and human potential to be a happy person—an individual who will see each moment as glorious and beautiful as the golden, glowing sunset at the end of a busy, fulfilling, fleeting day.

Over a period of time, study your weaknesses and strengths. Observe and record your behavior in relation to your powerful boss. Determine if there were specific actions that seemed to be beneficial or which hindered progress. Firmly stamp on your memory, with its solid elasticity, those actions that helped; stamp them into your mind and subconscious, as firmly as the notary public's hand-embossed seal on the legal document. Recall these experiences as needed for future survival purposes.

With each unpleasant situation, determine if fear, anger, worry, or depression is your resultant reaction. This will help you get to the deep root of the problem, which is as firmly entrenched in your subconscious.

Fear will be evident if you sense a vague, overpowering feeling of doom which gnaws at your stomach. There also can be a scary shadow associated with your employment world, a shadow that increases in reality with the appearance of your boss.

It is conceivable that you can adequately conquer fear of your employer—a fear that resides in the deep crevices of your mind, a fear that resembles a polluted, mountain stream, its purity completely contaminated with poisonous chemicals, rusty Coke cans, and other infectious debris.

You can usurp your fear by replacing it with a beautiful faith in yourself, resembling the application of a shiny wax job to a previously dirty, dull surface of an old Ford compact car. To accomplish this feat, read positive, attitude-building literature and stories of successful winners in their professional lives who have squelched their fears into the realm of nonexistence. Select cheerful material as opposed to something depressing. Your mind will absorb this pleasant, written content like a blotter soaking up a coffee spill.

Fear in and of itself is structured like a sinister, bleak, over-powering, looming shadow which many times has no firm, realistic foundation. It can be as unrealistic and tenacious as untruthful gossip which grows with extended usage. In some instances, fear is an increased reflection of a minor event, similar to the magnification of a tiny object when placed under a micro-scope. Because of its lack of importance, this shadow of fear will disappear if you stand up and face it. It will become as nonexis-tent as a disappearing bubble that gracefully floats into the atmos-phere and bursts into nothingness.

Many of our movies, television shows, and novels center their themes on unhappy, defeated individuals. Instead of satiat-ing your mind with such depressing material, read and watch only positive, enriching accounts of courageous individuals who have conquered huge hurdles. Completely immerse yourself with these stimulating, enthusiastic accounts; absorb them as thoroughly as a dried, black-eyed pea soaking up moisture from a pan of clear, cool water. These refreshing, true stories will recondition your mental framework. You will develop a solid positive attitude for your professional life. In addition, you will build a beautiful, reinforced faith in yourself. You will have renewed vigor, physical energy, and staunch determination.

Watch your reactions with your boss. Determine if this individual creates fear within you. If this is a reality, practice during your nonworking hours, visualizing yourself as conversing and interacting in a positive manner with your employer—but absolutely free of this characteristic fear. Courageously attack your fear like a brave German Shepherd dog assaulting a murderous burglar who is ransacking an expensive home. Contemplate your attack. Visualize. Visualize. Visualize. Realistically feel the fear floating out of your mind like a white, fluffy cloud which gracefully glides through a clear, blue sky.

When you dispel your burden of fear, you will feel as though you have been blessed with freedom from a prison dungeon with unconquerable walls of rock and iron. Renewed, enriching, physical energy will replace your previously exhausted physical condition. You will develop bundles of life-maintaining power.

Perhaps your reactions to your boss's behavior create righteous indignation as well as fear. You can tell if anger has swamped your subconscious when you wrathfully hold onto a thought, refusing to dismiss it, like a mighty bulldog who won't let go of its hapless victim.

You can adequately cope with fear. Consistently say to your subconscious, "Is my employer's behavior really worth the impairment of my emotional health and well-being?"

When you become angry, get to the root of the problem. Immediately detect the event that caused the attack. Assertively talk to your boss about his reaction and the anger that it causes in you.

In addition, when you are ill-humored, talk confidentially with a friend. With this technique, force your anger out of existence, like water that is turned into steam by compelling heat.

If you have no one with whom to converse, the next best approach is to write about your feelings. Thoroughly record in a diary every detail. By so doing, your mind will sense a release of the anger and allow your subconscious freedom, which it justifyingly deserves—freedom similar to that experienced by the zoo lion who suddenly escapes from his prison of iron bars.

Your behavioral reactions of fear and anger may be clouded by depression. Indications of this malady at a more serious level include a prolonged unhappiness, decreased bodily reactions, and unrealistic, hated, self-criticism. Depression of a milder degree can be evidenced by feelings of discouragement, isolation, and inferiority.

The individual experiencing either mild or serious depression has a feeling of hopelessness and anxiety similar to one who has undergone a profound loss. There is absolutely no enthusiasm for attacking a job. Life is seen as disheartening. Instead of energetically advancing into each new day with sureness, the person reacts with irritable, angry, or sad moods.

In addition to your fear, anger, and depression, you may be experiencing worry about your boss's reactions. Drive these worried thoughts out by saturating your mind with a positive attitude.

Practice. Practice. Practice. Practice cultivating friendships with cheerful, agreeable people who possess positive attitudes. Cultivate these friendships like a farmer who plants good seed, fertilizes it, and adds water. It is amazing the effect that other individual's attitudes can have on your own mental outlook and disposition.

You have developed the worry habit through practice, like the repetitive act of the nail biter who keeps his nails chewed to the quick. You can break the worry habit with concentrated, positive thinking. Substitute pleasant thoughts for the ones of worry. Whenever you exhibit concern, visualize this thought as floating out of your mind.

Coping Key Number Three: Understanding Your Boss

Your boss's distasteful reaction may stem completely from his/her personality and not from a dislike of you. Do not jump to the conclusion that your employer does not like you. This would be similar to a hasty leap executed by a frightened bullfrog, who, unfortunately, lands in a thorny bush. This disaster could have been prevented had the frog investigated the situation with more forethought and vision.

Study your employer's behavior thoroughly. Describe it in written detail, comparable to the scientist as he/she records the behavior or reaction of the organism under investigation.

Determine if your boss is reacting toward others as he/she does toward you. If this is true, then the problem resides in his/her unique personality and not in his/her relationship with you.

Next, look at the checklists in Part III. If you can identify his/her personality, then, at the bottom of the page, read how you can best function under this leader. If you are unable to adequately identify his/her behavior with use of the checklists, then your boss's disposition may be the result of a mixture of personality types.

To further understand your employer, make a study of the leadership style that he/she utilizes. Again, look at the appropriate checklist in Part III, which will assist you in this endeavor. If your boss does not portray a definite pattern, there may be a mixture of leadership styles. This crosses the lines of demarcation and prevents easy identification.

Coping Key Number Four: Defining the Problem

When tackling a problem with your boss, look at it with a thankful attitude. You possess the talent to solve the perplexities that come your way. Remember that you will never have a problem so large that you cannot conquer it with your endowed ability to cope—like an explorer who is victorious over new, exciting, and challenging territories. Visualize yourself in a detective role, a skilled, private investigator obtaining pertinent clues which fit neatly into place with given time, solving the problem at hand.

It is a specific fact that there will be individuals in this world with whom you experience difficulty. If you are as unfortunate as the wet, soaked, pussycat who gets caught in a rainstorm and have a troublesome boss, the best policy is to accept him/her for what he/she is. Spend your efforts in trying to understand his/her personality rather than trying to change him/her.

In defining your problem, religiously assemble the facts on paper, like the bank cashier who consistently records the amount collected for money orders. Objectively stand back as an observer. Look at the problem from the outside, as does an astrologer who views the stars in the heavens from his perch on Mother Earth. By so doing, you eliminate the situation from the biased, subjective realm.

First write down the general problem. Underneath it, record the specific perplexities. To give you an example of what is meant, see the following:

> General: I dislike my boss's actions
> Specifics:
>   a. Lies
>   b. Excessive authority which minimizes my freedom to
>   function independently

There is a purpose behind defining your problem. This material will be of value at a later date when you are developing positive affirmations in which you address these specific points.

As you work on solving your obnoxious problems, tension and anxiety may creep into your mind like a thief slipping into an enticing jewelry store with its lure of diamonds and emeralds. If you experience stress, this will stifle your freedom of thought power.

The manner in which you view your problem is of extreme importance. Immediately cast out negative thoughts, like a lizard who sheds his outer skin. Begin constructive work on your attitude promptly, comparable to the building crew who makes the architect's plan a reality. Your positive thoughts should encompass the fact that a problem will not continue forever. Eventually a solution will be within sight, just as a fiction story ultimately has a conclusion.

Survey your problem. Dissect it into organized portions, like an entomological student dismembering an insect for further study. View the perplexity in its entirety, like the driver who looks at the whole map in order to obtain an estimation of the mileage of his anticipated trip. Write this information down on paper to more fully impress every detail on your mind.

Put life's productive energy and optimism into your work, comparable to an artist whose abundant eagerness serves to keep him working on his beige canvas. Consistently train your mind to savor your work. Train. Train. Train.

Do not adopt the inaccurate viewpoint that you alone bear the weight of the world heaped upon your shoulders. Completely reject this false attitude allowing it to fly away as smoothly as a kite that sails into the blue heavens on a windy day.

Coping Key Number Five: Take Specific Action

The action you initiate today will become the realistic future.

Begin a program and successfully change your situation. Have confidence that you can excel. Do not ever lose sight of this fact.

Do not tackle your complete workload at one time. Establish high priorities: list the most crucial task in the first-place position, and the least in final place. Next, effectively arrange the remaining jobs in the appropriate priority.

In your diary, constantly, faithfully record your thoughts over an extended period of time, comparable to the actions of a bookkeeper who consistently registers financial items underneath the debit or credit column.

At the end of each day, count the times you have had unpleasant thoughts as opposed to positive ones. If your poor-thought ledger is longer, you are fostering an inordinate amount of negative thoughts into your subconscious, just like poisonous chemicals being slowly accumulated over time in the human body, causing it to deteriorate into a cancerous condition.

Keep in mind that your plan of action is completely up to you, resembling the authority that the captain has in directing his ship in time of war.

It is true that you will feel a huge crescendo of relief when you acknowledge that you possess the key that will unlock your door of happiness—a key you can either intelligently utilize or allow to lay concealed under a collection of negative thoughts and rubbish.

In your diary, consistently record situations that are threatening to you in your relationship with your boss—threatening like a black, angry-looking cloud hovering over Mother Earth. The more of these threatening situations you anticipate, the better you will be able to positively respond.

Continue taking immediate, pertinent action!

Do not become like the boat in the harbor which remains in one spot because it is minus a motor. The cost of accomplishment demands valuable time and productive energy, allowing the wings of your belief to eloquently fly.

As you progress, problems will surface. Don't let these difficulties squelch you like a fire that destroys a new building. Conquer these new problems with a positive attitude. Firmly attack each problem as it appears. Do not allow them to accumulate.

Utilize your diary for self-monitoring purposes, identifying your reactions to frustrating situations. Did you handle them positively or negatively? With this tool, determine if consistent behavior-action models are originating.

On a separate sheet of paper and utilizing your ever-faithful diary, differentiate between the times in which polite assertiveness should have been applied as opposed to those in which you should have reacted wholeheartedly to your boss's requests.

After surveying the information in your diary, define your objectives. Chart your job-orientation directions like a navigator charting a ship's course on his map.

With your diary, write down the major items that need improvement. Then, underneath these, write the behavioral steps that you will follow to reach this goal. Utilize the following one as an example:

Goal: To feel less tension in the presence of my boss
Methods to utilize:
    1. Relax each portion of my body when my boss appears
    2. Visualize floating to a peaceful place.

Coping Key Number Six:
Incorporate a Relaxation Program

Normally, whenever you have a problem with your boss, you will experience a specific amount of stress. On such occasions it is crucial to relax.

Relaxing will necessitate a long period of effort when you are in the beginning stage. However, do not become disheartened. This involves the development of a new ability. For a full grasp, it is necessary to devote an extensive amount of time equal in scope to the hours required for learning balance techniques in riding a bicycle.

The exercises in this section are strategic if the worry of your job is creating sleep problems. Complete mastery of them will serve as the best sleeping pill you have ever digested.

After mastering these techniques, if you still discover difficulty in relaxing, then perhaps a licensed psychologist's biofeedback program would be advantageous. Utilize the following relaxation exercises:

1. Recline comfortably in a chair or on a sofa or bed.
2. Totally submit yourself to this piece of furniture.
3. Deeply breathe. Satiate your lungs with rejuvenating air, allowing it to seep into the inner portion. This has been achieved when your abdomen, below your stomach, expands and contracts.
4. Visualize each portion of your human shell as tension free. Visualize. Visualize. Visualize. Consecutively tense and relax voluntary muscles. Work specifically on one part of your body. For example, tense your right foot. See this condition by affirming, "My right foot is tense." Think about how your foot feels in this condition. Then release the tension. Also accompany this by saying, "My right foot is relaxed." Observe the differentiation in the way your foot now

feels as opposed to tightness. Next progress to your left foot, right leg, left leg, hips, shoulders, and forehead until you have traversed your total body with these relaxation methods. Now picture yourself in a tension-free state.
5. Consecutively tense and relax your total body.
6. Close your eyes. See yourself floating to a serene place, like a Hawaiian shoreline. Land at this peaceful spot by relaxedly soaring on a soft, billowy cloud which suspends you in the atmosphere. Picture yourself resting contentedly on the beach. Smell the cool, delightful, ocean air. Feel the soft, warm sand as it glides through your fingers. Hear the white-capped, mighty waves as they hit the rough, rocky shoreline a short distance down the beach.
7. Check on your muscles. Determine if they are in a relaxed condition. If not, repeat your previous exercises.

On a tiny sheet of paper concisely list the prior relaxation techniques for utilization at work. Your brief inventory could read as follows:

1. Deeply breathe;
2. Relax each muscle;
3. Visualize total body as relaxed;
4. See yourself gliding to a peaceful place;
5. Picture a tranquil scene.

Utilizing your diary, make a list of tension indicators. Continually watch for stress cues in your work-a-day world. Add to your original list new stress provokers that appear. Consistency in this endeavor—yes, consistency—is what will pay its full measure of reward.

Coping Key Number Seven: Develop Good Habits

Initiate a program of daily physical exercise. This will stimulate the blood flow to various parts of your body, enriching your cells and assisting in eliminating waste chemicals. As a result, your power to think and sense will increase. Physical relaxation will spread to your muscles, like a blanket of yeast gradually penetrating every portion of raw dough. If physical exercises are completed one hour before retiring, they will serve as an effective sleeping pill, luring you into an environment of sound sleep.

Take time out for recreation. This will help in leading your mental sphere away from the stressful day at work. Recreation does not have to bear a price tag. Do something that you enjoy. This consecutive practice will recharge your human battery, supplying it with renewed energy.

Straighten up your bodily posture. Walk with calm peacefulness. This will help rejuvenate a depleted confidence level.

Coping Key Number Eight: Develop Positive Thinking

Your power reserve has only started to be utilized. Psychologists indicate that we use only a tiny degree of our abilities. Individuals who have convinced themselves about their inaccurate supply of talents are restrained not because of physical limitations, but because of their structured mental attitude.

One of the most powerful of all phenomena is the human mind—the storehouse for the subconscious. This mechanism directs your entire existence. It is like a mirror which reflects your experience and knowledge. When your conscious mind rigidly absorbs an idea, good or bad, it is transferred to the subconscious, resembling data programmed into a computer which is then stored away in its memory for future recall.

Firmly retain the thought that what you accomplish in your employment setting is comprehensively dependent on your perception of it—not on the actual job itself. Therefore, it is urgent to tell your subconscious the correct thing, for if inaccurate information is perceived and relayed to your inner mind, then this mechanism believes a falsehood. It cannot differentiate between what is true or incorrect. In turn, this belief, whether it be true or false, has the power to pilot your behavior, like the wind whose power steers the expensive, white-and-blue sailboat.

Therefore, view your work with accuracy. Ponder over it, like the research scientist who thoroughly studies what chemical to apply next to his basic solution.

Develop positive, healthy perceptions. These will point and keep you along the right path of life, just as a pilot who has the ultimate power over a magnificent jet. Dismiss erroneous facts before they embrace you, as prison walls secure the hardened criminal.

You can accomplish those goals that you think you can. You alone have this crucial key!

It is a psychological fact that if a person overly anticipates a problem or thinks the worse, it is then consumed by the subconscious. The expected perplexity then gains the potency to expose itself into the world of reality. This applies equally to your job. Believe that you can eliminate the problems of your job and that is exactly what you will do. Nourish and positively ice your professional world like the cook who places a delicious, rich topping on the surface of a yummy chocolate cake, finishing it in gourmet style.

The following poem is applicable at this point:

> If you think you are beaten, you are;
> If you think you dare not, you don't;
> If you want to win but think you can't,
> It's almost a cinch you won't.
>
> If you think you'll lose, you've lost;
> For out in the world we find,
> Success begins with a fellow's will;
> It's all in the state of mind.
>
> Life's battles don't always go
> To the stronger and faster man.
> But sooner or later the man who wins
> Is the man who thinks he can.
>
> —Walter D. Wintle

Attaining mental peacefulness requires concentrated, industrious cultivation. When you have gained this resource, you will have expanded intellectual talent and physical energy. This gift, this asset, will benefit you in weathering every employment storm.

If you have been conquered by a perplexity in your job, it could well be that you have stressed to your subconscious the impossibility of this situation. By so doing, you have emphasized the negative rather than the positive. In turn, if you have sold your inner, mental sphere on this idea, you are setting yourself up for failure.

Since anything negative has a powerful influence on your subconscious, it is imperative to eradicate negative words such as "can't," "should," "ought to," "wish," "might," and "must." These words can be both the result and cause of worry, resembling a rotten apple that ruins the entire crate—becoming both the instigator and finisher of the otherwise delectable fruit.

Words are a powerful motivating force. Therefore, if you will eliminate these negative hindrances, you will have a mind packed with peace—peace like that existing in a beautiful area in a forest near a fast-flowing stream with crystal-clear, bubbly water, pure enough to drink.

If gloomy words constantly cloud your inner mind, they will thwart and defeat you. For example, when you allow the "can't" thought to occupy your subconscious, then you establish a ripe environment for "can't" to develop.

You have the power to eliminate negative words and put positive ones in their stead. Retain this crucial fact. Diligently watch your overt speech, listing the words that need to be discarded from your conversation and thoughts. Place the list in an obvious location, like on the refrigerator door. Every morning, to jog your memory, inspect your list.

Underneath your negative words, list peace-enriching words like "tranquil" and "serene." In addition, review these each morning, instilling them within your thoughts throughout the entire day.

Practice imagining positively. Practice. Practice. Practice. At ten intervals during your working day engulf your inner mind with peace-loving thoughts. Visualize these positive thoughts as completely filling your mental sphere and flowing over the side of your subconscious pot like hot tea running over a cup's rim and down to the saucer. If cheerful thoughts inhabit your mind, unpleasant ones will not have space to enter, for your consciousness will be filled to capacity with a positive attitude.

At work, establish a regular program for positive imagery. Initially, be certain that your body is relaxed, using the techniques previously described. Using your watch as a reminder, every hour take a few moments to visualize happy words. In addition, during the hectic, rushed portion of your working day, relax comfortably in your chair and chase the negative thoughts from your mind—like the shepherd who drives away the lion from his herd of peaceful, loving sheep. As this trash rushes from your mind, picture yourself in a totally calm state at a serene place, such as a cabin in a heavily wooded, mountain resort.

Coping Key Number Nine:
Develop Positive Self-talk Affirmations

Look at your original chart which lists your problem areas with its general and specific goals. From this list, identify positive affirmations that you can utilize in talking to your subconscious, giving it the optimistic support that it needs. To clarify, you affirm something to your inner, mental sphere when you state firmly that you will do a specific thing. You can develop control of your thoughts with a positive viewpoint.

For your assistance in developing positive affirmations, the following are given as an example. Utilize these to develop those which are applicable to your situation:

SELF-TALK AFFIRMATIONS TO CONTROL STRESS AND TENSION

1. I will change my life by constantly directing my thought structure.

2. I have the supremacy of my mind to preserve inner peace
   therein.
3. My life is a beautiful, beneficial one.
4. In order to relieve tension I will:
   a. speak confidentially with a friend talking it out of my
      system;
   b. make daily notations for frustration-venting purposes in
      my diary.
5. I will progress one step at a time with my problem.

SELF-TALK AFFIRMATIONS TO CONTROL FEAR AND ANGER

1. I will reduce my fear of my boss until it is completely relieved.
2. When possible, I will laugh about a frustrating situation.

SELF-TALK AFFIRMATIONS TO CONTROL DEPRESSION

1. I will constantly remember pleasant events from the past.
2. I will not allow my boss's attitude to affect me in the least
   way.

SELF-TALK AFFIRMATIONS TO PROMOTE SLEEP

1. I will incorporate relaxation methods to develop better sleeping habits.
2. I will feel relaxed in my entire body.
3. Tension will vanish from my body and mind.
4. Tonight I will sleep well.
5. In the morning I will awaken with a refreshed spirit, bound-
   ing with enthusiasm.

DEVELOP FAITH AND WIN

If you will incorporate the previous ideas, you will develop
a beautiful faith which will not be easily defeated. This asset is
the strategic ingredient!

Insulate and pad your zeal with a positive mental outlook,

resembling insulation securing walls against the penetration of an icy, winter wind.

When your faith increases, your self-confidence level will, in turn, grow. It will have a circulating effect. The more of this trait you have, the more victories will be attained. These will then increase your level of confidence.

Faith in yourself will increase happiness and enthusiasm. What you do in your job is largely dependent on the energy generated toward what you are doing—an energy which is possible only with the backing of a positive mind.

Individuals who have jumped high life-hurdles—comparable to the Olympic athlete who transcends and conquers his/her obstacles—seem to be charged by a super battery of optimistic faith. This beautiful attitude adequately equips such individuals with plentiful, energetic supplies for performing even an almost impossible feat.

A beautiful faith in yourself as an individual is the key that will unlock your professional door. Develop this and you will assuredly be the winner in the final analysis. With it, nothing can conquer you—no matter what adversity comes your way.

Faith! Faith! Faith! Yes, faith in yourself is the answer. With this asset you can conquer your employment problems and arise victoriously—a winner!

PART III
PERSONALITY AND LEADERSHIP CHECKLISTS

INTRODUCTION TO PART III: APPENDICES

It is dangerous to stringently classify personality and leadership with too narrow a frame of reference. Both of these entities are extremely complex; neither are ever simple or cut-and-dry.

However, as leadership becomes more extreme and progresses well within the range of either dictatorial or democratic, it becomes more easily distinguishable.

The same thing can be said relative to personality. The more excessive the behavioral trait, the more identifiable it is. Books in psychology do, generally speaking, place personality within specific areas with trait labels in order to more adequately handle this complex aspect of the psyche. Likewise, these same labels have been utilized in these personality checklists and in previous discussions of bosses.

Leadership style is affected by personality. Generally speaking, the better adjusted and more secure the individual boss, the easier it will be for him/her to grant freedom to his/her employees within a democratic environment.

In contrast, dictator-like, autocratic bosses will more than likely feel insecure and dislike their personalities, causing them to projectively dislike some aspects in their employees' personalities. Their insecurity will not grant them the right to give freedom to their employees. They will, in turn, expect complete obedience to their every dictate and command.

The *laissez-faire* bosses, who do not care one way or the other, will more than likely grant freedom to their employees. However, they will not administer the necessary leadership and guidance.

Since personality does affect leadership, each individual situation needs to be analyzed separately to determine if the boss's reign would be democratic, dictatorial, or *laissez-faire*.

The type of personality traits that are needed in a good leader are, in part, a function of the specific situation. Therefore, the behavior of leaders will vary considerably from one employment environment to another.

Another factor of importance is the personality of the employee. This will determine what sort of leadership is most effective for the individual. Employees low in the desire for independence who wish to know exactly what is expected of them through precise instructions will function best under dictatorial bosses. Those high in the need for independence will do better under democratic leadership.

In the following pages, there is a checklist for determining a boss's leadership style, whether dictatorial, democratic, or *laissez-faire*. There is another checklist to determine *your* preference for these styles of leadership. The last set of checklists identify bosses with specific personality characteristics and the technique for an employee's survival skills under each type of leadership.

If you find no checklist that specifically describes your boss, he/she may be exhibiting a mixture of personality characteristics. As indicated earlier, personality is complex and may not fit neatly into any one of these areas.

Appendix I. Checklists

LEADERSHIP STYLES OF BOSSES

The three checklists on the following pages have been designed to help you in determining which leadership style your boss is exerting—dictatorial, democratic, or *laissez-faire*.

The more checks there are under a specific style, the more a boss is functioning within that framework.

Dictatorial Boss Checklist

_________Possesses rigidity in opinions and points of view;

_________Views personality in a simple manner, as normal or abnormal, with no in-between, average range;

_________Places entire working environment under strict domination and tolerates no deviation from it, demanding that employees adhere with strict obedience to regulations;

_________Emphasizes importance of authority;

_________Spends excessive time manipulating situations for his own best interests;

_________Exhibits extreme dislike and prejudice in relationships with employees, especially toward those who deviate from his/her authority;

________Possesses unquestioning respect of and submission to superiors;

________Prefers simple and obvious solutions to problems;

________Possesses dislike for unpredictable situations;

________Dislikes suggestion for changes presented by employees and discourages this endeavor;

________Directs the behavior of employees toward predetermined goals;

________Feels that he/she possesses far more knowledge than his/her employees;

________Criticizes and belittles employees;

________Likes work that is clear and well understood;

________Has a tendency to stereotype employees, placing them within a certain mold and refusing to change his/her mind, even when presented with new information;

________Prefers the attribute of conformity in employees;

________Feels an extreme need for order;

________Likes regularly established routines;

________Bullies employees;

________Blames own inadequacies on employees;

________Complains of imaginery threats, coming especially from specific employees;

_________Feels specific employees are inferior;

_________Shows extreme negative attitudes toward certain employees;

_________Makes every decision;

_________Feels employees are either with him/her or against him/her, accepting no intermediate feelings;

_________Shows an almost paranoid tendency to feel that certain employees are out to destroy him/her;

_________Displays a toughness, steering clear of expression of emotions;

_________Attributes his/her craving for power to others, projecting this need on to certain employees, accusing them of this tendency and of trying to usurp his/her power.

Democratic Boss Checklist

_________Likes employees who can adequately function independently;

_________Likes employees who will carry out and fulfill responsibilities;

_________Likes employees who will bring in new and innovative ideas;

_________Grants freedom to function to employees;

_________Is excellent at delegating responsibility to employees;

_________Friendly;

________Warm;

________Supportive of employees;

________Will intervene for well-deserving employees when expedient to justly protect their rights;

________Does not manipulate his/her employees;

________Adjusts quickly to change in plans and is not disturbed by it;

________Feels no prejudice toward employees;

________Does not place employee's personality into a specific, stereotyped mold;

________Agrees that personality is complex;

________Welcomes suggestions for change from employees;

________Never dominates employees;

________Does not bully employees;

________Feels security within himself/herself and therefore is able to give freedom to employees.

Laissez-faire Boss Checklist

________Passive;

________Indifferent;

________Unhelpful;

__________Leaves employees alone, never interfering;

__________Causes work of employees to progress in a haphazard fashion and at a slow pace;

__________Promotes unproductive activity;

__________A considerable amount of arguing exists between employees;

__________Has minimum communication with employees;

__________Employees lack a sufficient flow of ideas and suggestions from their leadership.

Appendix II. Checklists

STYLES OF
LEADERSHIP PREFERENCE

The three checklists on the following pages have been designed to help you in determining which type of boss you prefer—dictatorial, democratic, or *laissez-faire*.

The more checks there are under a specific style, the more you enjoy working for that type of boss.

Employee Who Will Function Well
under Dictatorial Boss

__________Obediently follows every command of boss;

__________Likes a working environment which is simple;

__________Never questions boss's decisions;

__________Never makes suggestions for changes;

__________Totally conforming and submissive;

__________Keeps desk in a neat, well-ordered fashion;

__________Never leaves the impression that he/she is threatening boss;

__________Reserved;

_________Subservient;

_________Extremely respectful toward boss's authority;

_________Is able to place boss on a pedestal;

_________Is able to make boss feel important;

_________Never places boss in a situation in which he/she has to defend himself/herself.

In summarizing, employees will effectively function under dictatorial bosses with total loyalty and respect, with few questions relative to their employment world. Employees should not function independently without permission, nor should they give their bosses reasons to feel threatened.

Employee Who Will Function Well
under Democratic Boss

_________Is able to function independently without overpowering supervision;

_________Has creative ideas and wants to convey these suggestions for changes to others;

_________Feels security in a situation that is not tightly structured;

_________Willingly accepts responsibility.

In summarizing, employees can effectively function under democratic bosses if they have initiative to complete their work independently. Bosses with these leadership styles will create environments that stimulate creativity in employees and grant freedom to function.

These bosses can best be handled by employees who exert initiative in their respective areas. They can feel free to communicate new ideas designating improvement changes.

Employee Who Will Function Well under *Laissez-faire* Boss

________Prefers indifferent, passive boss;

________Prefers boss who ignores employees;

________Works well under a haphazard, disorganized situation;

________Does not mind colleagues who spend excessive time arguing;

________Satisfied with boss's lack of communication with employees.

In summarizing, employees who effectively function under *laissez-faire* bosses are those who are content with no apparent changes in their employment world. These bosses will require tip-top patience for they contentedly will be happy with no improvements. Employees of these bosses will function efficiently if they do not expect their suggestions to be incorporated.

Appendix III. Checklists

DESIGNED FOR BOSSES
WITH SPECIFIC
PERSONALITY PROBLEMS AND
HOW AN EMPLOYEE
CAN LEARN TO FUNCTION WELL
UNDER SUCH A BOSS

Psychologically, the bosses depicted in this appendix are not neurotic and definitely not psychotic. They possess personality problems that are less severe and produce less anxiety. These personality perplexities are discussed within the pages of numerous books on psychology.

The more checks there are under a specific style, the more of this characteristic would be displayed by your boss.

Hysterical Personality

_________Seeks attention;

_________Likes to play a dramatizing role;

_________Is vain, egocentric, and egotistical;

_________Has shallow feelings;

________Frequently seen as seductive and may behave in a sexually provocative way, using this as an attention-getting device;

________Overreacts to minor stresses with exaggerated emotional displays;

________Attempts to influence the behavior of colleagues and friends in order to meet some desired, self-imposed goal;

________Likes commonplace things, like material wealth;

________Places emphasis on making contact with important people upon whom he/she may rely to obtain a favored position;

________Masters the mechanics of obtaining the center of attention;

________Exhibits outward opposition—when it is safe;

________Avoids taking an unpopular stand;

________Depends heavily upon others for approval;

________Makes excessive demands on friends;

________Has immature ways of speaking and acting;

________Displays wishful thinking;

________When frustrated, can become quickly angry;

________May be impulsive and unreliable;

________Feels no need to be exact or on time;

________Will enter a social gathering late in order to make a dramatic entrance;

________Will purchase the most expensive home or car just for impression purposes;

________Lacks accuracy in his/her statements; for example, "That's what I meant and you should have known it.";

________Outward social appearance is important;

________Tends to imitate the behavior of those he/she considers important;

________Places emphasis on being a member of the "inside group";

________Will exclude individuals who are different, looking at them with disdain;

________Seeks friends and cannot risk isolation;

________Usually friendly, social, and talkative; however, may be shy should the situation warrant it;

________Likes excitement and wants to be the center of it as long as this will risk no uncomfortable consequences.

It is likely that bosses of this type might exert dictatorial leadership styles because they like to be the center of attention.

Employees will work better under these bosses if they are sincerely complimentary. Respond to their social needs by volunteering assistance at socials. Remain calm in the face of their overreactions, which consist of exaggerated emotional displays in response to minor stresses. Be friendly, for these bosses will probably, in most cases, respond to this. Also, tolerate and overlook their immaturity and impulsiveness. Also be tolerant of the inaccuracy and related confusion in their statements, such as "You should have known what I meant."

Employees will effectively function if they will ignore their bosses' shallow feelings, their vain, egotistical personalities, and their sexually provocative mannerisms.

It is more conducive to allow these bosses total authority with few questions relative to the employment world. Proceed with leadership when asked by these employers.

Paranoid Personality

_________Is defensive in order to protect himself/herself;

_________Constantly safeguards himself/herself against attack, either slight or large, either imagined or real;

_________Hypersensitive to slights (real or imagined);

_________May magnify unconscious hostility in other people;

_________May assume that what is clear to him/her will be clear to others;

_________Lacks basic trust and may be suspicious, jealous, and obstinate;

_________Sees others as disliking him/her;

_________Inability to tolerate criticism without resentment;

_________Alert in his/her relationships with people for indications that will confirm his/her innate suspicion that others dislike him/her;

________Makes few friends;

________Guards his/her private world;

________May utilize specific measures in order to protect himself/ herself, like changing locks on doors as a matter of precaution from time to time;

________Interpersonal relationships are usually unhappy;

________May be busy defending himself/herself and seems inconsiderate.

Because of their suspiciousness, these bosses will probably be more of the dictatorial types.

Employees will function best under these leaders if they are careful not to offend. Handle these bosses carefully! Keep a stiff upper lip. Do not let their hypersensitive attitudes bother you. Be careful not to leave the impression that you are questioning their decisions. In addition, do not leave the impression that you are criticizing them. Do not be shocked at their need to change locks or make other strange gestures in order to protect themselves in their private little worlds.

Obsessive-Compulsive Personality

________Has an excessive need for conformity;

________May be rigid;

________May be overconscientious;

________May not be able to relax easily;

________May dislike unclear and unpredictable situations;

________Unpredictable conditions may create anxiety;

_________Likes to organize his/her life, down to the smallest of details;

_________Prefers not to take chances;

_________Prefers to plan ahead of time and not leave until the last minute;

_________May see himself/herself as responsible for anything that happens;

_________Feels the desperate need to control his/her environment as well as himself/herself;

_________Feels anxiety when things are out of control;

_________Rituals may be appealing and he/she may utilize this technique for controlling his/her world, such as religiously checking—time and again—a stack of papers to determine if things are in order;

_________Tries to be correct, strives for perfection;

_________May analyze and examine tiny statements in an argument in order to protect himself/herself;

_________Works better in a structured, organized environment where he/she can maintain control;

_________If his/her situation depends on the temperamental mood changes of his/her boss, he/she may become anxious and fearful;

_________May offend employees because of his/her extreme attention to detail;

_________Is unable to delegate responsibility, feeling the compulsive need to do everything himself/herself;

__________Is a hard worker who may outwardly seem trustworthy and responsible;

__________Expects perfection from his/her employees;

__________Has workaholic tendencies.

This boss will probably be more of the dictatorial type because of his/her need to control everything in the environment.

You will function best under this boss if you are careful about specific details of your job. Have your paperwork well organized in minute detail. Have things planned well in advance, never leaving the impression of unclear situations or that things are out of control. Do not become offended because of your boss's inability to delegate responsibility.

As this employer will usually not delegate authority in handling tasks, do things in a peripheral way that will be of assistance. This will require considerable innovativeness on your part. In addition, casually volunteer your time and effort for specific tasks. Your boss will usually be appreciative, allowing you to help where otherwise he would not have delegated this authority. Since this boss strives for perfection, if you complete these tasks exceptionally well, this will satisfy his perfectionistic feathers. Also it will lead him to develop confidence in you. As a result, he may allow you to perform other tasks in a more independent way.

Schizoid Personality

__________Seems to be a "loner" and seclusive, with little desire for companionship; has a tendency to avoid close or prolonged relationships;

__________Does not expect to find a real place in the social world, retreating from it to some private corner; functions as

a social isolate, as if he/she were trying to shelter him-
self/herself from others;

__________Seems aloof and disinterested;

__________Appears to be living in an ivory tower; a detached and
abstract thinker;

__________Uncomfortable with others;

__________Excessive time may be spent daydreaming;

__________Cannot express hostility;

__________Unsatisfying to hold a conversation with him/her for
he/she makes little effort to keep the communication
going;

__________Is secretive and does not talk about himself/herself, in
order to maintain his/her privacy;

__________Never feels fully accepted;

__________Avoids competitive relationships;

__________Appears odd or snobbish;

__________May give the appearance of being self-sufficient;

__________May become a recluse who lives in a little room and
seldom speaks to anyone;

__________Especially uncomfortable around members of the oppo-
site sex; seldom dates.

The boss with this personality may be more *laissez-faire* than
dictatorial or democratic.

Employees can best handle this boss by not desiring a close relationship. Allow this leader the seclusiveness that he/she needs. Work around this characteristic. Do not delve into his/her inner, private life. Accept his/her need to avoid competitive relationships. If you are a member of the opposite sex, accept his/her uncomfortableness without question. If possible, help put him/her at ease by being relaxed and cheerful. Offer to be of assistance in completing special tasks, especially those that require considerable contact with others.

Manic-Depressive Personality

__________Switches quickly from a mood that is enthusiastic and optimistic to one that is grouchy and depressed;

__________Inconsistently temperamental;

__________Difficult to judge from one day to the next what mood will be displayed;

__________Following a tense situation, he/she may become excessively elated and happy;

__________May, at times, be easily distracted; not an adequate listener;

__________May, at times, be unable to remain with a task for a lengthy period of time, instead continuing in a constant state of shifting from one task to another;

__________May, at times, shout very loudly and excitedly when talking to another individual, either in person or over the telephone;

__________May, at times, overreact when such a strong display of emotion is not justified;

_________May, at times, be excessively talkative, creating difficulty for another person attempting to enter into the conversation;

_________May, at times, jump from one topic to another;

_________His/her above behaviors do not correspond to the appropriate situations, either at work or in a social setting.

This boss's leadership style may jump from one extreme to another. It may quickly go from democratic to dictatorial, depending on the mood he/she is experiencing. When a happy mood occurs, democratic leadership may appear. However, when in a depressed mood, he/she may wield strict authority and become dictatorial.

An employee will get along better with this boss if he/she is able to adjust to a constant change in mood from happiness to depression. Do not let his/her distraction and short attention span unnerve you. Do not let his/her overreaction be of major concern. If he/she jumps from one topic to another, listen and enter into the conversation when appropriate. When your boss is excessively talkative, listen.

Inadequate Personality

_________May give inappropriate responses to emotional, social, and physical demands at work;

_________May display inadaptability and lack of responsibility;

_________May use poor judgment;

_________May lack physical stamina;

_________May cause himself/herself or others to fail at some task.

This boss's leadership style will more than likely completely lack guidance. Therefore, it will probably swing more toward the *laissez-faire* realm, with an almost "I don't care" attitude.

An employee will function best if he/she does not expect this boss to accept responsibility for his/her actions. This employer may not "go to bat" for an employee when in reality this is deserved and justified. Accept the fact that although this boss says he/she will do something, it may never be accomplished.

BIBLIOGRAPHY

Adams, Henry E. *Psychology of Adjustment*. New York, New York: The Ronald Press Co., 1972.

Adorno, T. W., Else Frenkel-Brunswik, D. J. Levinson, and R. N. Sanford. *The Authoritarian Personality*. New York, New York: Harper and Row, 1950.

Allport, G. W. *ABC's of Scapegoating*. Chicago, Ill.: Central Y.M.C.A. College, 1944.

Atkinson, John W. *Personality, Motivation and Action—Selected Papers*. New York, New York: Praeger Publishers, 1983.

Azrin, N. H., R. R. Hutchinson, and D. F. Hake. "Extinction—Induced Agression." In *Roots of Aggression–A Re-examination of the Frustration-Aggression Hypothesis*. Ed. Leonard Berkowitz. New York, New York: Atherton Press, 1969, pp. 35–60.

Baldwin, John D. and Janice I. Baldwin. *Behavior Principles in Everyday Life*. Englewood Cliffs, New Jersey: Prentice-Hall, Inc., 1981.

Bastick, Tony. *Intuition—How We Think and Act*. New York, New York: John Wiley and Sons, 1982.

Baughman, E. Earl. *Personality—The Psychological Study of the Individual*. Englewood Cliffs, New Jersey: Prentice-Hall, Inc., 1972.

Bernard, Harold W. and Wesley C. Huckins. *Dynamics of Personal Adjustment*. 3rd ed. Boston, Mass.: Holbrook Press, Inc., 1975.

Blank, Leonard and Kenneth Lewes. *Psychology for Everyday Living*. New York, New York: Mayflower Books, 1980.

Bradburn, Norman M. with the assistance of C. Edward Noll. *The Structure of Psychological Well-Being*. Chicago, Ill.: Aldine Publishing Co., 1969.

Brennecke, John H. and Robert G. Amick. *Psychology and Human Experience*. Beverly Hills, Calif.: Glencoe Press, 1974. (Photographs by Claire Steinberg/Illustrations by Robert Ronketti.)

Brown, Roger and Richard J. Herrnstein. *Psychology*. Boston, Mass.: Little, Brown and Co., 1975.

Bruno, Frank. *Adjustment and Personal Growth: Seven Pathways.* 2nd ed. New York, New York: John Wiley and Sons, 1977.

Bugelski, B. Richard and Anthony M. Graziano. *The Handbook of Practical Psychology.* Englewood Cliffs, New Jersey: Prentice-Hall, Inc., 1980.

Burtt, Harold Ernest. *Applied Psychology*. 5th ed. Englewood Cliffs, New Jersey: Prentice-Hall, Inc., 1964.

Candland, Douglas K., Joseph P. Fell, Ernest Keen, Alan I. Leshner, Roger M. Tarpy, and Robert Plutchik. *Emotion.* Monterey, Calif.: Brooks/Cole Publishing Co., 1977.

Chein, Isidor. "The Awareness of Self and the Structure of the Ego." In *Understanding Human Motivation*. Eds. Chalmers L. Stacey and Manfred F. DeMartino. Revised ed. New York, New York: The World Publishing Co., 1965, pp. 292, 289, 290.

Coan, Richard W. *The Optimal Personality*. New York, New York: Columbia University Press, 1974.

Davids, Anthony and Trygg Engen. *Introductory Psychology*. New York, New York: Random House, 1975.

Dollard, John, Leonard W. Doob, Neal E. Miller, O. H. Mowrer, and Robert R. Sears. "Frustration and Aggression." In *The Dynamics of Aggression (Individual, Group, and International Analyses)*. Eds. Edwin I. Megargee and Jack E. Hokanson. New York, New York: Harper and Row, Publishers, 1970, pp. 22, 25, 26, 27, 30–32.

Erb, Everett D. and Douglas Hooker. *The Psychology of the Emerging Self*. Philadelphia, Pa.: F. A. Davis Co., 1967.

Ewen, Robert B. *An Introduction to Theories of Personality*. New York, New York: Academic Press, 1980.

Fadiman, James and Robert Frager. *Personality and Personal Growth*. New York, New York: Harper and Row, Publishers, 1976.

Fischer, William F. *Theories of Anxiety*. New York, New York: Harper and Row, Publishers, 1970.

Fitch, Stanley K. *Insights into Human Behavior*. Boston, Mass.: Holbrook Press, 1970.

Gaylin, Willard, M.D. *Feelings: Our Vital Signs*. New York, New York: Harper and Row, Publishers, 1979.

Gilmer, B. von Haller. *Applied Psychology—Adjustments in Living and Work*. New York, New York: McGraw-Hill Book Co., 1975.

Goodstein, Leonard D. and Richard I. Lanyon. *Adjustment, Behavior and Personality*. Reading, Mass.: Addison-Wesley Publishing Co., 1975.

Grasha, Anthony F. and Daniel S. Kirschenbaum. *Psychology of Adjustment and Competence—An Applied Approach*. Cambridge, Mass.: Winthrop Publishers, Inc., 1980.

Gulley, Halbert E. and Dale G. Leathers. *Communication and Group Process Techniques for Improving the Quality of Small-Group Communication*. 3rd ed. New York, New York: Holt, Rinehart and Winston, 1977.

Hall, Calvin S. and Gardner Lindzey. *Theories of Personality*. 2nd ed. New York, New York: John Wiley and Sons, Inc., 1970.

Harcum, E. Rae. *Psychology for Daily Living*. Chicago, Ill.: Nelson-Hall, 1979.

Harlow, Harry F., James L. McGaugh, and Richard F. Thompson. *Psychology*. San Francisco, Calif.: Albion Publishing Co., 1971.

Harrison, Albert A. *Individuals and Groups—Understanding Social Behavior*. Monterey, Calif.: Brooks/Cole Publishing Co., 1976.

Hepner, Harry Walker. *Psychology Applied to Life and Work*. 6th ed. Englewood Cliffs, New Jersey: Prentice-Hall, Inc., 1979.

Hershey, Gerald L. and James O. Lugo. *Living Psychology An Experimental Approach*. London, England: The Macmillan Co.—Collier-Macmillan Limited, 1970.

Hilgard, Ernest R., Richard C. Atkinson, and Rita L. Atkinson. *Introduction to Psychology*. 6th ed. New York, New York: Harcourt Brace Jovanovich, Inc., 1975.

Hill, Winfred F. *Psychology—Principles and Problems*. Philadelphia, Pa.: J. B. Lippincott Co., 1970.

Holland, Morris K. *Psychology, An Introduction to Human Behavior.* Lexington, Mass.: Heath, 1974. (Designed and illustrated by Milton Zolotow.)

Hunter, Edward. *Brainwashing.* Linden, New Jersey: The Bookmailer, Inc., 1965.

Izard, Carroll E. *Emotions in Personality and Psychopathology.* New York, New York: Plenum Press, 1979.

Izard, Carroll E. *The Face of Emotion.* New York, New York: Appleton-Century-Crofts, 1971.

Izard, Carroll E. *Human Emotions.* New York, New York: Plenum Press, 1977.

Izard, Carroll E. (with chapters coauthored by Edmund S. Bartlett and Alan G. Marshall). *Patterns of Emotions.* New York, New York: Academic Press, 1972.

Keen, Ernest. "Emotion in Personality Theory." In *Emotion.* Eds. Douglas K. Candland, Joseph P. Fell, Ernest Keen, Alan I. Leshner, Roger M. Tarpy, and Robert Plutchik. Monterey, Calif.: Brooks/Cole Publishing Co., 1977, pp. 225, 228, 229, 230, 233, 238, 240, 242, 243, 246.

Klein, George S. *Perception, Motives and Personality.* New York, New York: Alfred A. Knopf, 1970.

Krasner, Leonard and Leonard P. Ullmann. *Behavior Influence and Personality: The Social Matrix of Human Action.* New York, New York: Holt, Rinehart and Winston, Inc., 1973.

Lamberth, John, John C. McCullers, and Roger L. Mellgren. *Foundations of Psychology.* New York, New York: Harper and Row, 1976.

Lasswell, Harold D. *Power and Personality.* New York, New York: W. W. Norton and Co., Inc., 1976.

Levitt, Eugene E. *The Psychology of Anxiety.* 2nd ed. Hillsdale, New Jersey: Lawrence Erlbaum Associates, Publishers, 1980.

Lindgren, Henry Clan and Donn Byrne. *Psychology: An Introduction to a Behavioral Science.* 4th ed. New York, New York: John Wiley and Sons, Inc., 1975.

Lindgren, Henry Clay and Leonard W. Fisk, Jr. *Psychology of Personal Development.* 3rd ed. New York, New York: John Wiley and Sons., Inc., 1976.

Lindzey, Gardner, Calvin S. Hall, and Richard F. Thompson. *Psychology*. New York, New York: Worth Publishers, Inc., 1975.

Lyons, William. *Emotion*. Cambridge and London, England: Cambridge University Press, 1980.

McKeachie, Wilbert James, Charlotte Lackner Doyle, and Mary Margaret Moffett. *Psychology*. 3rd ed. Reading, Mass.: Addison-Wesley Publishing Co., 1976.

McMahon, Frank B. (Boxes by Judith W. McMahon.) *Psychology: The Hybrid Science*. 3rd ed. Englewood Cliffs, New Jersey: Prentice-Hall, Inc., 1977.

Mandler, George. *Mind and Emotion*. New York, New York: John Wiley and Sons, Inc., 1975.

Martin, David G. *Personality Effective and Ineffective*. Monterey, Calif.: Brooks/Cole Publishing Co., 1976.

Mednick, Sarnoff A., Jerry Higgins, and Jack Kirschenbaum. *Psychology Explorations in Behavior and Experience*. New York, New York: John Wiley and Sons, Inc., 1975.

Mischel, Walter. *Introduction to Personality*. 2nd ed. New York, New York: Holt, Rinehart and Winston, 1971.

Robbins, Lewis L. "Unconscious Motivation," In *Understanding Human Motivation*. Eds. Chalmers L. Stacey and Manfred F. DeMartino. Revised ed. New York, New York: The World Publishing Co., 1965, pg. 389.

Robinson, Daniel N. *Psychology, Traditions and Perspectives*. New York, New York: D. Van Nostrand Co., 1976.

Rosenthal, R. and L. Jacobsen. *Pygmalion in the Classroom: Teacher Expectation and Pupils' Intellectual Development*. New York, New York: Holt, Rinehart and Winston, 1968.

Rubinstein, Joseph. *The Study of Psychology*. Guilford, Conn.: The Dushkin Publishing Group, Inc., 1975.

Ruch, Floyd L., Vytautas J. Bieliauskas, John L. Fuller, Eugene H. Galanter, Harry F. Harlow, Robert W. Russell, J. P. Guilford, and Saul B. Sells. *Psychology and Life*. 6th ed. Chicago, Ill.: Scott, Foresman and Co., 1963.

Sartain, Aaron Quinn, Alvin John North, Jack Roy Strange, and Harold Martin Chapman. *Psychology: Understanding Human Behavior*. 3rd ed. New York, New York: McGraw-Hill Book Co., 1967.

Schein, Edgar H. "The Chinese Indoctrination Program for
    Prisoners of War: A Study of Attempted 'Brainwashing'." In
    Readings for an Introduction to Psychology. Ed. Richard A. King.
    New York, New York: McGraw-Hill Book Co., 1966, pp.
    447-473.

Scott, John Paul. *Aggression*. 2nd ed., revised and expanded.
    Chicago, Ill.: The University of Chicago Press, 1975.

Senter, R. J. and Richard E. Dimond. *Psychology: The Exploration
    of Human Behavior*. Glenview, Ill.: Scott, Foresman and Co.,
    1976.

Sherman, Mark. *Personality Inquiry and Application*. New York,
    New York: Pergamon Press, 1979.

Silverman, Robert E. *Psychology*. 2nd ed. Englewood Cliffs, New
    Jersey: Prentice-Hall, Inc., 1974.

Sjöbäck, Hans. *The Psychoanalytic Theory of Defensive Processes*.
    New York, New York: John Wiley and Sons, 1973.

Spivack, George, Jerome J. Platt, and Myrna B. Shure. *The
    Problem-Solving Approach to Adjustment—A Guide to Research and
    Intervention*. San Francisco, Calif.: Jossey-Bass Publishers,
    1976.

Strongman, K. T. *The Psychology of Emotion*. New York, New
    York: John Wiley and Sons, 1973.

Taylor, Dalmas A. and Sidney A. Manning. *Psychology: A New
    Perspective*. Cambridge, Mass.: Winthrop Publishers, Inc.,
    1975.

Taylor, David A. *Mind*. New York, New York: Simon and
    Schuster, 1982.

Verdier, Paul A. *Brainwashing and the Cults—An Exposé on
    Capturing the Human Mind*. North Hollywood, Calif.: Wilshire
    Book Co., 1977.

Vernon, Walter M. *Introductory Psychology*. Chicago, Ill.: Rand
    McNally College Publishing Co., 1976.

Voss, James F. *Psychology As a Behavioral Science*. Pacific Palisades,
    Calif.: Goodyear Publishing Co., Inc., 1974.

Weiner, Bernard. *Theories of Motivation from Mechanism to
    Cognition*. Chicago, Ill.: Markham Publishing Co., 1972.

Whaley, Donald L. and Richard W. Malott. *Elementary Principles of Behavior*. Englewood Cliffs, New Jersey: Prentice-Hall, Inc., 1971.

Whittaker, James O. *Psychology*. Philadelphia, Pa.: W. B. Saunders Co., 1970.

Wiggins, Jerry S., K. Edward Renner, Gerald L. Clore, and Richard J. Rose. *Principles of Personality*. Reading, Mass.: Addison-Wesley Publishing Co., 1971.

Wintle, Walter D. "Thinking." *The World's Best-Loved Poems*. Ed. James Gilchrist Lawson. New York, New York: Harper and Row, 1927, pg. 116.

Wishard, J. Kenneth. *Techniques of Leadership*. New York, New York: Vantage Press, 1965.

Zillmann, Dolf. *Hostility and Aggression*. Hillsdale, New Jersey: Lawrence Erlbaum Associates, Publishers, 1979.